WOMEN WHO COUNT

WOMEN WHO COUNT

BY SHELLY M. JONES, PH.D.

ILLUSTRATED BY VERONICA MARTINS

2010 *Mathematics Subject Classification*. Primary 97A30, 97U99.

For additional information and updates on this book, visit
www.ams.org/bookpages/mbk-124

Library of Congress Cataloging-in-Publication Data

Names: Jones, Shelly M., 1964- author.
Title: Women who count : honoring African American women mathematicians / Shelly M. Jones.
Description: Providence, Rhode Island : American Mathematical Society, [2019] | Includes bibliographical references.
Identifiers: LCCN 2019013589 | ISBN 9781470448899 (alk. paper)
Subjects: LCSH: Women mathematicians–United States–Biography. | African American women–Biography. | African American mathematicians–Biography. | Mathematicians–United States–Biography. | AMS: Mathematics education – General, mathematics and education – History of mathematics and mathematics education. msc | Mathematics education – Educational material and media, educational technology – None of the above, but in this section. msc
Classification: LCC QA27.5 .J67 2019 | DDC 510.92/52–dc23
LC record available at https://lccn.loc.gov/2019013589

Dedicated to the memory of Aunt Joan and Uncle Bill

Contents

Acknowledgments   ix
Introduction   xi

The Mathematicians   *The Activities*

Chapter 1: The Firsts   1

Dr. Martha Euphemia Lofton Haynes   African American Women Mathematicians   2
    Connect the Coordinate Points

Dr. Evelyn Boyd Granville   Color the Mercury Friendship 7 Spacecraft   6
    NASA Facts

Dr. Marjorie Lee Browne   Color by Shape!   10
    Geometry Vocabulary Word Search

Chapter 2: The Pioneers   15

Dr. Sylvia Trimble Bozeman   Fun with Magic Squares   16
    Euler Graphs: Paths and Circuits

Dr. Etta Zuber Falconer   Sisters Chapel Coloring   20
    Magic Squares Challenge

Dr. Sadie Catherine Gasaway   Color By Number   24

Dr. Gloria F. Gilmer   Color Me Pretty!   26
    What's That Word?

Dr. Gloria Conyers Hewitt   Teaching Children is What I Love! Coloring Page   30
    Lucky You! Word Search

Dr. Genevieve Madeline Knight   Dr. Genevieve Knight Maze   34
    Decode the Puzzle

Dr. Carol E. Malloy   Find the Treasure Chest   38
    Benjamin Banneker Gears

Dr. Vivienne Lucille Malone-Mayes   Tangram Coloring   42
    Making Tangram Figures
    Mystery Shape Equations

Dr. Argelia Velez-Rodriguez   Cuban Street Scene Coloring Page   48
    Fraction Facts: Color the Planets

Chapter 3: The Un-Hidden Figures   53

Dr. Christine Mann Darden   Dr. Christine Darden Crossword Puzzle   54
    Tessellation Darden
    Sudoku Puzzle Fun

Mary Winston Jackson   Brain Buster   60
    Wind Tunnel Math

Katherine Coleman Goble Johnson   Katherine Johnson Riddle   64
    Katherine Johnson Word Search

Dorothy Johnson Vaughan   Color the Fish Tessellation   68
    Decode the Message about Dorothy Vaughan
    Quadrilateral Transformations

Chapter 4: The Contemporary Firsts   73

Dr. Christina Eubanks-Turner   Pattern Block Design   74

Dr. Raegan Higgins   Integer Race   76

Dr. Tasha R. Inniss   Dr. Tasha Inniss's Message   78

Dr. Monica Jackson   Spatial Statistics Map   80

Dr. Talea Mayo   Palindrome Magic!   82

Dr. Yolanda Parker   Lemon Pi(e)   84

Dr. Candice Price   Solve the Shapes Puzzle   86

                                    Mathematics and More Crossword Puzzle

Dr. Shree W. Taylor   Dr. Taylor Word Search   90

Dr. Erica N. Walker   Flower Creative Coloring   92

Dr. Chelsea Walton   Function Fun Word Search   94

Dr. Talitha M. Washington   Blast Off! Plot the Points   96

Dr. Kimberly S. Weems   Statistics Words to Know   98

Dr. Shelby Wilson   I Spy   100

Selected Activity Answer Keys   103

References   129

About the Author   133

About the Illustrator   135

Photo Credits   137

Acknowledgments

The stories of African American women mathematicians have long been hidden. Although there have been some people over the last four decades highlighting the accomplishments of these women, until recently they have remained in the shadows. Fortunately, in the last few years there has been an awakening to the positive narratives of African American women mathematicians that hold promise in encouraging more girls to study mathematics and to seek careers in the mathematical sciences. In acknowledging the people who made this book possible, I would like to start by paying homage to the women honored therein. Each of their individual and collective journeys has inspired me.

During my research, I contacted many people in the mathematics community, and I am thankful for their contributions. They include Drs. Edray Herber Goins, the late Rudy Horne, Johnny Lott, Erica N. Walker, Talitha M. Washington, the creators of the *Mathematically Gifted & Black* website (Erica Graham, Raegan Higgins, Candice Price, and Shelby Wilson), and Scott W. Williams, who created the *Mathematicians of the African Diaspora* website. I especially want to thank Drs. Sylvia T. Bozeman and Gloria Conyers Hewitt for speaking with me about their experiences as mathematicians. I was inspired by Margot Lee Shetterly's *Hidden Figures* and encouraged by my colleague Sara MacSorley, author of *Super Cool Scientist*.

Thank you to my illustrator Veronica Martins, who has done a magnificent job sketching the portraits of the Firsts, the Pioneers, the Un-Hidden Figures, and the mathematician featured on the book cover. Thank you to Brea Ratliff for designing the mathematicians' pages and Donald Collins for designing the book cover. Thanks to all the contributors to the book, including Elise Archibald, Sabrina Doolgar, Kristen Jados, Lindsey Lampognana, Tony Mahfoud, Katherine Nemer, Reilly Slavin, and Gavriela Ziu-Pires. Thank you to Gwen Brantley and the students at Access Educational Services, Inc., the National Coalition of 100 Black Women New Haven Metropolitan Chapter, and students at Ross Woodward Classical Studies Interdistrict Magnet School in New Haven, CT, for testing many of the book's activities. Mr. Eldorado Anderson, your Black Wall Street events are tremendous.

Thank you, Sandy Harden, for your friendship and expertise in editing and photography. Thank you, Be Chan, Lindsay Keazer, David LaPierre, Dr. Maria Mitchell, Dr. Mary Anne Nunn, Dr. Gail Nordmoe, Tatyana Rivera, MJ Terry, and Wayne Winston, for your contributions. I appreciate the support of my friends Regina Spears-Cuffee, Yolanda Jones, and Marissa Artis. Cousin Summer Lowe, hair stylist extraordinaire, you always make me look my best.

Thank you to all my Kickstarter backers, especially the late A. Jewell Strother who lovingly nudged me to "finish the book" and those who have supported me through donations, books sales, and supportive comments. Dunn Pearson, Jr., you have been there from day one on this project and have encouraged me along the way. Thank you for your love and constant support.

Finally, I'd like to thank my family who has supported me in all my endeavors. My daughters Brelynn Brown and Brooklynn Brown, you are the inspiration for all that I do. My siblings Mary Roacher, Sanya Roacher, John Jones, Jr., and Jason Jones, Sr., you are always there to help out. My parents John Jones, Sr., and Arlene Jones, you are the best parents anyone can ask for. I love you all.

I can do all things through Christ who strengthens me. Philippians 4:13

Introduction

I have spent my entire career as a mathematics educator helping students make sense of mathematics by showing them the structure of mathematics and by having them explore mathematical concepts. When students are able to recognize the patterns and connections within mathematics, they begin to see the beauty of mathematics and its relevance. As a result they gain confidence in themselves as doers of mathematics. I am passionate about my work as a mathematics educator. Through my work and advocacy, I will to continue to inspire students to become empowered through mathematics.

As an African American woman and a mathematics educator, I was inspired by the book and movie *Hidden Figures* to write this book, *Women Who Count: Honoring African American Women Mathematicians*. The book aims to continue to bring attention to the positive narratives of African American women in mathematics, including their contributions to mathematics and glimpses into their personal lives as well.

In selecting the mathematicians for this book, I consulted personal contacts in the mathematics community as well as website resources such as *Mathematicians of the African Diaspora: Black Women in Mathematics* and *Mathematically Gifted & Black*. My selection criteria for choosing the women in the book was that they each earned at least one degree in mathematics and that they used mathematics in their careers.

The format of this book includes a portrait sketch or picture and a short biography for each of the mathematicians, as well as elementary- and middle-school activities including word searches, crossword puzzles, unscrambling mathematics vocabulary, solving equations, and more. The book is divided into four sections of mathematicians. The first section, entitled The Firsts, includes the first three African American women to earn doctorates in mathematics: Drs. Martha Euphemia Lofton Haynes, Evelyn Boyd Granville, and Marjorie Lee Browne. The second section, entitled The Pioneers, includes nine African American women mathematicians who laid the groundwork and became role models for future mathematicians. The third section, entitled The Un-Hidden Figures, includes four distinguished women whose lives were chronicled in the book *Hidden Figures* by Margot Lee Shetterly. These women, among many others, played significant roles in the space race as they were "human computers" at the National Aeronautical Space Administration (NASA). The fourth and final section, entitled The Contemporary Firsts, includes 13 mathematicians who are at the beginning and midpoint stages of their careers. These twenty-first-century mathematicians are breaking barriers by becoming firsts in their universities and companies. For example, Dr. Talitha M. Washington learned that she was the first African American female to earn a doctorate in mathematics from the University of Connecticut in 2001.

A Message to Teachers:

I am deeply concerned that many children from underrepresented groups do not see themselves as mathematicians. This is partly because they are not exposed to mathematicians that look like them, and therefore they lack the necessary role models. When Margaret R. Sáraco [43] asked her middle school students to name some mathematicians from history, "they had difficulty coming up with five names. And of those five mathematicians named, none were female or minority" (p. 70). On the other hand, when students were asked to name a favorite athlete, actor, or musician, they could name many and knew all kinds of information about these role models. Sáraco goes on to say that "if we have our young scholars research men and women who have made contributions to the field of mathematics, they may find a role model" (p. 75).

Research suggests that successful African American women mathematicians have several attributes in common. In their early years, they had family members who believed in them and supportive teachers who specifically told them that they could be mathematicians [25]. Later in the students' academic careers, they reported being successful due to having role models and mentors [9]. *Women Who Count* seeks to increase students' knowledge of successful minority women in mathematics, thus providing them with role models that have the potential to significantly impact their lives.

A Message to Parents and Students:

I am proud to have the opportunity to share the stories of these 29 extraordinary women so that students can benefit from learning about a variety of occupational fields related to mathematics. One of the issues that parents face is how to motivate their children to succeed in mathematics. Through reading this book, parents will gain information they can use to support their children and to encourage them to be successful in mathematics.

In this book you will read about careers in astronomy and space exploration through the lives of the Un-Hidden Figures of NASA, Christine Darden, Mary Jackson, Katherine Johnson, and Dorothy Vaughan. You will also read about Dr. Talea Mayo's work in climate study, where she uses data to improve models that help predict floods caused by hurricanes. Among many other stories, you will also read about Dr. Monica Jackson's research, which includes spatial statistics and disease surveillance. Students will benefit from reading about these careers because it will open their minds to new ways of thinking about mathematics outside of what they may have previously known.

Students, you may use this book as a springboard into the world of mathematics. Have you ever heard of a magic square, a tessellation, or sudoku? If the answer is yes, then you might want to challenge yourself by solving these activities on your own. If you've never done these types of activities, you may ask for help from a parent, family member, friend, or teacher. If you are creative, you can color the flower in the book so that it shows symmetry. If you prefer I Spy, the book includes that as well. There is something for everyone in this book. Have fun doing the activities, but don't forget to read and learn about these wonderful women who happen to love mathematics! After reading their stories, continue to seek out other positive role models in STEM-related careers (Science, Technology, Engineering, and Mathematics).

I hope you enjoy the book!

Sincerely,

Shelly M. Jones, Ph.D.

Chapter 1: The Firsts

Dr. Martha Euphemia Lofton Haynes

The first African American woman to earn a Ph.D. in mathematics.

Martha Euphemia Lofton was born in 1890 and lived in Washington, DC, all her life. Euphemia, as most people knew her, was the daughter of a dentist, Dr. William S. Lofton, and his wife Lavinia Day Lofton. Euphemia was a lifelong advocate for providing better opportunities for students in the poorer neighborhoods, and she was concerned about the segregated neighborhoods. She graduated from Washington's Miner Normal School in 1909 and then earned a bachelor's degree in mathematics from Smith College in 1914. Smith is a women's college in Northampton, Massachusetts.

After she earned her B.A. degree she returned to DC, where she married childhood friend Harold Appo Haynes. Dr. Haynes's husband was also involved in education and was the deputy superintendent for DC's "colored schools". As involved as they both were with education, they had no children.

Although she lived most of her life in DC, she traveled to different parts of the country to continue her studies. She earned a master's degree in education from the University of Chicago and then returned to DC to earn a Ph.D. in mathematics from Catholic University of America in 1943.

After receiving her master's degree, she joined the faculty of Miner Teachers College, which stressed training African American teachers. She created the mathematics department at Miner. While at Miner she enjoyed teaching different grade levels and different topics. At different times, she taught first grade at Garrison School and English at Miner College, as well as being a professor at Miner Teachers College.

After nearly 50 years as an educator Dr. Haynes retired in 1959. She became the president of the Board of Education and was central to the integration of DC public schools.

In retirement, Dr. Haynes continued to work for several causes and organizations, including the Urban League and the National Association for the Advancement of Colored People (NAACP), fighting racial segregation. She was also a member of the Council of Catholic Women and the American Association of University Women. Dr. Haynes was very involved in her church and was awarded the Papal Medal from the Catholic Church.

After she died it was discovered she had left $700,000 to Catholic University of America to continue her work in the education department and to provide scholarships to students to continue their educations.

She died in 1980 at the age of 89.

African American Women Mathematicians

```
M Y K Q R Z B Y K H U M H Y T G V W Z D
H B U T E O P R A K M Q D V A V D U K K
E C L H W G D Y W Y E A C Y C S Z M R F
W A N G T C N R W D E I O Z U N Y U U H
I G F I M E P B I R Z J U P H N H I U U
T K Z N S A R O C G G Z R E B M E O Y N
T V I K Q O L C L V U E H K Y L B B Y T
R M N C W B M L N Z N E E S L A T R H N
B N P N S P E Q O O I V Z I T U B P X B
R A E P E E G P C Y Q E V P L W C E P
V M A T N K C L V I T N R D X Q Y P M Y
Z E O B U V A M E V A Q E M V N N O Y F
A Z H Q N F A F G R A X G O G E O P Y S
D O B E F Y O R G Y J L A A X D T U W T
E B J R E O U E W A O H V U G R T H G Q
A T V S P Q G M V W N M S J X A U T I I
T M N P M M B L K A E N J R F D S Q P T
M K F U M I Q I Y S S H U E S E I M S E
X Y T C H B T G W A T S O N U I K H O N
A O T Z G Q D H G G R K S P I K E S N W
```

WORD LIST:

BOZEMAN	GIPSON	KNIGHT	SPIKES
BROWNE	GRANVILLE	MALLOY	SUTTON
DARDEN	HAYNES	MAYES	SVAGER
FALCONER	HEWITT	MCBAY	WATSON
GASAWAY	HUNT	MCCREADY	
GEE	HUNTE	RODRIGUEZ	
GILMER	JONES	SMITH	

Connect the Coordinate Points

Using the map below and the coordinate plane, complete the following tasks:

Task 1

Using a dark pencil, plot the following points and connect them in the order that they are plotted. This will provide you with the outline of Washington, DC.

(-6.5, 3.8); (-1.2, 9); (7.2, 0); (-1, -9); (-1, -5);
(-0.8, -4); (-1.5, -2); (-6.5, 3.8)

Task 2

Use a different colored pencil for each location below. Plot and label the points representing the schools that Dr. Haynes attended or taught at in Washington, DC.

    A. Armstrong High School: Point A (0.5, 1.5)
    B. Catholic University of America: Point B (1.5, 4.5)
    C. M Street High School: Point C (0.5, 2)
    D. Miner Normal School: Point D (-0.3, 2.5)
    E. Miner Teachers College (University of District of Columbia):
        Point E (-3.5, 4.5)
    F. Smith College: Point F (-1.5, 2.5)

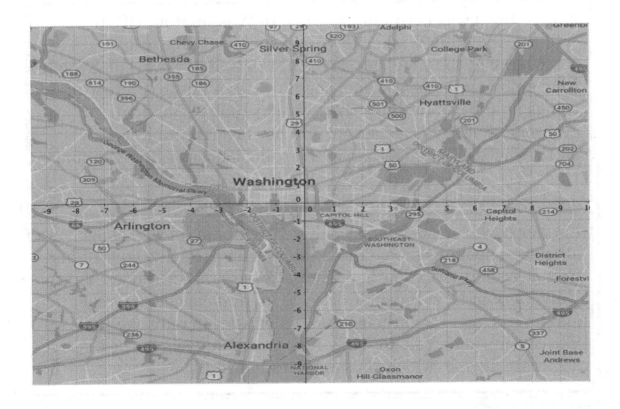

Dr. Evelyn Boyd Granville

The second African American woman to earn a Ph.D. in mathematics.

Evelyn Boyd was born May 1, 1924, in Washington, DC, to William and Julia Walker Boyd. Washington, DC, was segregated at the time, but as a child that didn't prevent Evelyn from enjoying the books from the libraries and the interesting things at all the museums that were available. She told everyone that she loved school and her favorite subject was math. She graduated as one of five valedictorians from Dunbar High School.

For her bachelor's degree, she chose to attend Smith College, an all-girls school in Northampton, Massachusetts. She earned her first degree in 1945. For her graduate work, she attended Yale University in New Haven, Connecticut, and earned a double master's degree in mathematics and physics in only one year. She continued at Yale to study functional analysis for her doctorate degree, which she completed in 1949.

After graduating she became a mathematics professor at Fisk University in Nashville, Tennessee. Fisk is a historically Black university and was formally called The Fisk Freed Colored School. Both Vivienne Malone-Mayes and Etta Zuber Falconer (also in this book) enjoyed her classes and later, under her influence, earned doctorate degrees in mathematics. Willing to try new experiences, Boyd temporarily left teaching and went to work at the National Bureau of Standards (later renamed the Diamond Ordnance Fuze Laboratories), where she worked on developing fuel for rocket ships. After four years in that position she moved to New York City to take a position at IBM (International Business Machines) as a computer programmer. One of Dr. Granville's most interesting jobs was when she went back to Washington, DC, to work as part of the IBM team responsible for the formulation of orbit computations and computer procedures for NASA's Projects Vanguard and Mercury.

In 1960 she met and married her first husband, and they moved to California. She worked with several companies in the aviation business but eventually became an assistant professor of mathematics at California State University in Los Angeles (CSULA). At CSULA she was very involved in training future teachers on how to teach mathematics in elementary-school classrooms. This interest in teaching math encouraged her to coauthor a college mathematics textbook for future teachers.

In 1984, she married Edward V. Granville and moved to Tyler, Texas, where she embarked on a 30-year career as a professor at Texas College. She was a professor of computer science. While teaching at Texas College she, and her husband, raised 800 chickens and sold their eggs.

In 1989, Dr. Granville was awarded an honorary doctorate degree from Smith College, the first one given by an American college to an African American woman in mathematics. She received a second honorary doctorate degree from Spelman College in 2006.

Dr. Evelyn Boyd Granville was a mathematician, computer scientist, and educator. After her retirement in 1997, she continued to be involved with mathematics by encouraging students to explore the value of mathematics, as well as serving as a national speaker for many different associations. When someone asked her what she thought her biggest contribution to math was, she stated, "Being an African American woman, and letting people know that we have brains too".

Color the Mercury Friendship 7 Spacecraft

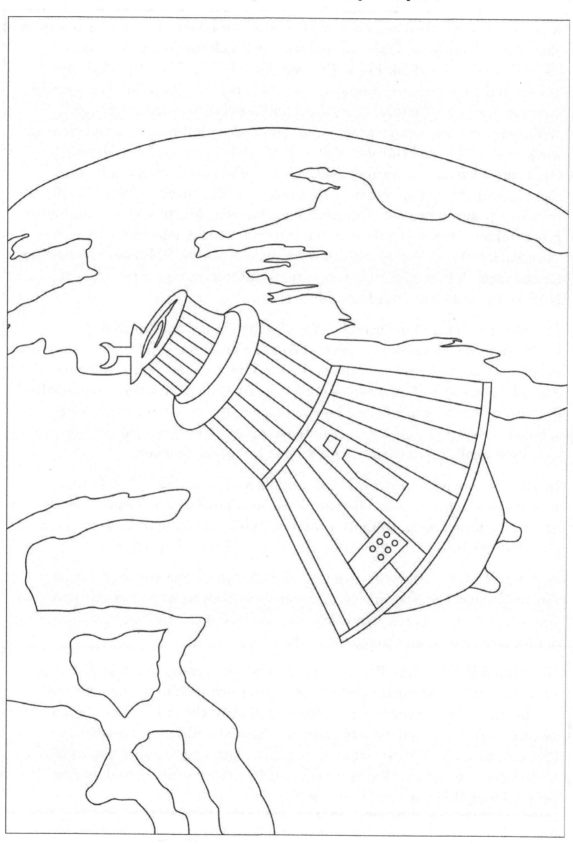

NASA Facts

What is the name of the oldest artificial satellite still in space today?

$$\frac{\text{V}}{1} \quad \frac{\quad}{23} \quad \frac{\quad}{19} \quad \frac{\quad}{5} \quad \frac{\quad}{11} \quad \frac{\quad}{13} \quad \frac{\quad}{12} \quad \frac{\quad}{4} \quad \frac{\quad}{7}$$

Which NASA program launched the first Americans into space?

$$\frac{\quad}{9} \quad \frac{\text{R}}{2} \quad \frac{\quad}{15} \quad \frac{\quad}{17} \quad \frac{\quad}{18} \quad \frac{\quad}{20} \quad \frac{\quad}{16} \quad \frac{\quad}{10} \quad \frac{\quad}{8} \quad \frac{\quad}{22} \quad \frac{\quad}{14} \quad \frac{\quad}{21} \quad \frac{\quad}{3} \quad \frac{\quad}{6}$$

To answer the questions, complete the following tasks for each problem below:
1. Work the problem (the first two are done for you).
2. Find the code for the correct answer.
3. Write the code in the blank space that corresponds to the problem number.

CODE	ANSWER
A	-27
B	2
C	4
D	5
E	-81
F	-2
G	-6
H	0
I	2.5
J	10
K	0.7
L	-55
M	-53
N	-4
O	34
P	55
Q	100
R	-21
S	-100
T	-14
U	20
V	1
W	-0.50
X	13
Y	-3
Z	-13
1	-51

1) $(-2) + 3 = 1$ (find 1 in the answer column, the code is V)
2) $(-14) + (-7) = -21$ (find -21 in the answer column, the code is R)
3) $-13 + (-8) =$
4) $(-9) + 14 =$
5) $(-8) - (-2) =$
6) $5 + (-8) =$
7) $(-27) - 24 =$
8) $(-41) + (-40) =$
9) $38 - (-17) =$
10) $(-44) + (-9) =$
11) $(-16) - (-36) =$
12) $(-6) - 15 =$
13) $(-16) - 6 + (-5) =$
14) $15 - 13 + 2 =$
15) $16 - (-13) - (-5) =$
16) $(-7) - (-2) - 9 =$
17) $(-11) - (-14) + 7 =$
18) $7 + (-1) - 6 - 81 =$
19) $6 + (-7) + (-5) - (-2) =$
20) $(-3) + 5 + (-5) + 7 =$
21) $(11) + 8 + 1 =$
22) $-10 + (-10) - 1 =$
23) $-6 - 5 - 16 =$

Dr. Marjorie Lee Browne

The third African American woman to earn a Ph.D. in mathematics.

Marjorie Lee was born September 9, 1914, in Memphis, Tennessee. Her parents were Lawrence Johnson Lee and Mary Taylor Lee. Marjorie's father had attended some college, which was something very unusual in 1914. Around their hometown, he was known as a whiz at mental mathematics, and he shared his enthusiasm with his children. Marjorie said she always loved mathematics. Growing up, Marjorie attended both public and private schools. Most notably she attended LeMoyne High School, a private school started after the Civil War by the Methodist Church to educate Negroes.

By the time she was old enough to go to college, the Great Depression had begun. With a combination of scholarships, jobs, and loans she was able to attend Howard University in Washington, DC. She graduated with honors with a bachelor's degree in mathematics from Howard University in 1935. After a brief teaching position at the Gilbert Academy in New Orleans, Louisiana, she received a master's degree from the University of Michigan in 1939. After earning her master's degree, she became a faculty member at Wiley College in Marshall, Texas. It was during that time she began working on her doctorate degree at the University of Michigan.

Dr. Browne received a Ph.D. in mathematics from the University of Michigan in 1950. This made her the third African American woman to receive a mathematics doctorate degree, just six months after Dr. Evelyn Boyd Granville. After receiving her Ph.D., Dr. Browne taught at North Carolina Central University (NCCU), the nation's first public liberal arts college founded for African Americans, located in Durham.

Browne's work offered her many opportunities to travel and teach. She even went to Cambridge University in England, where she studied topology. Topology is what happens when you change the shape of an object by bending and/or twisting. Topology is a type of geometry that became her specialty.

Dr. Browne became aware of the importance of the new field of computers. She applied for, and received, an IBM grant to set up a computer center. The computer center was one of the first for a minority college. Due to her work, the college became a National Science Foundation center for secondary education in mathematics. Because of her deep interest in continuing education for secondary school teachers, she continued to direct summer institutes for teachers for 13 years.

In addition to her work at NCCU, Dr. Browne belonged to many different organizations and received many awards. She worked at NCCU until the time of her death in 1979 at the young age of 65.

In 2001, the University of Michigan–Ann Arbor began a lecture series honoring Marjorie Lee Browne.

Color by Shape!

1. Color all 3-sided polygons green. What is the name of a 3-sided polygon?
    _____

2. Color all parallelograms with no right angles blue. Write the properties of a parallelogram. _____

3. Color all rhombi pink or purple (your choice). What is another name for these polygons? _____

4. Color all rectangles yellow. Are rectangles also parallelograms? How do you know? _____

5. Color all trapezoids red. Write the geometric properties of a trapezoid.

    _____

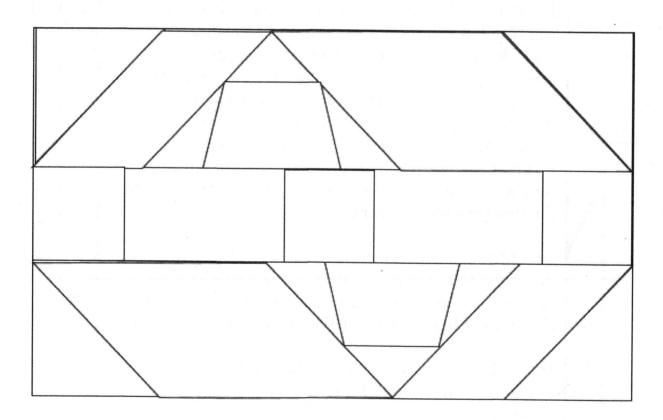

Geometry Vocabulary Word Search

Have fun finding interesting geometry vocabulary. Can you define each term?

```
                           J
                         B E J
                       R P I I X
                     S E C O S J R
                   V V D Z E L C Y E
                 V Z G N W W B Y L O G
               J D N W I T C Z C G A T U
             V O O S R L I I O E V O G E L
           Q D I U J Z Y F E F S R B N U L A
         C E T X O O F C X A D M Z A H Y U G R
       T R C L E C I D W U R U K D J U M G Y N M
     G E E T L Z L B J P A M M S A F K Q W N T A Q
   X H L R G S G Y A P P H G V D A K J B S C O I T P
 F P F A N Q T C R F R P H G R J I M K R R I V G A C Y
 T S E P A G J R D A M N E C C I K G A G V W T U J A F E H
 B A R E K C B B A Z V T N R T O L M P K W C Q C W C A X T R H
Z P B Z N Q A J B N W J O K P V A N P D K C V P W Q W E C E C B I
Y F K O G S C Y T B S N Q Z X E M R L G J C F L O E T F E N E H N T M
B Y G I Z I B L Q K Q V O V X G N F L D I R T X R B T C S T A T J M X N T
Z T N D V V O F A E X Y E G W W A D J Q M S U U E T S J I I K W J E T J U Z S
U R H I R H Y B Q I V R A B E E I P H G A L Q E X B B X L V O E H R H I C
G A V O L U M E X N S T J Y G C D V G B X C E N C A R E T E M I R E P
D N C D K D P A O A N U U X U S F Z Z K V U Y T B W U O N A A L X
Q S Z T W C A X L E N C F L J I L S X R A L I M I S O Y Y J E
A F Z K F A R H P Z X K A P C H W C M I H E M A I O P G E
W O X F U G A E U A L R S O M V Q C U A D J T Q B C L
R R Y P P F L K O O A L U M R O F H D R A M W S G
O M V N M N L S Y J E Z M Q O B C T L E Q R N
T A X J P H E S O C T A G O N W S X C A A
A T Y O A I L L B K O B P B N B Z E I
T I G J O H O R G S Z Y A Z N J R
I O C M E R G V D E R M E J T
O N W R H B R V T Y L D U
N U Y B Q B A Z D O J
Z B O T V I M E A
Z U R A Z M P
E N O C O
I L W
I
```

WORD LIST:

ANGLE	FORMULA	POLYGON	TRANSFORMATION
AREA BISECT	HEXAGON	RECTANGLE	TRANSLATION
CENTER CONE	OCTAGON	REFLECTION	TRANSVERSAL
CONGRUENT	PARALLELOGRAM	REGULAR	TRAPEZOID
CYLINDER	PENTAGON	ROTATION	TRIANGLE VOLUME
EQUILATERAL	PERIMETER	SIMILAR	
	PERPENDICULAR	SPHERE	
	PI	SQUARE	

13

Chapter 2: The Pioneers

Dr. Sylvia Trimble Bozeman

Dr. Sylvia Trimble Bozeman believes that there is no limit to what students can achieve if they are encouraged and supported.

Sylvia Trimble was born in 1947 in Camp Hill, Alabama, where she grew up on a farm as one of five children. Her parents valued education and passed on to her their love of learning and their belief in helping others. She also credits her dedicated high school teachers, who went far beyond what was required, for her early educational development. One of her teachers even came back after school and taught a small group of students trigonometry, which wasn't included in the regular curriculum. Like many others, during that time, she attended segregated schools.

Dr. Bozeman earned three degrees in mathematics: first, in 1968 she earned a bachelor of science from Alabama A&M University, a historically Black university in Huntsville; in 1971 she earned a master of arts from Vanderbilt University in Nashville, Tennessee; and in 1980 a Ph.D. from Emory University in Atlanta, Georgia. As she got more involved in the field of mathematics she realized that the field needed a more diverse population. Working to realize her dream to encourage underrepresented populations, she co-founded a national program, Enhancing Diversity in Graduate Education (EDGE), to assist women in making the transition to graduate school and in earning doctorate degrees in the mathematical sciences. The award-winning EDGE Program was developed with her colleague Rhonda Hughes at Bryn Mawr College in 1998.

Dr. Bozeman worked most of her career at Spelman College, where her past roles included chair of the department of mathematics and associate provost for science and mathematics. She retired from Spelman and is currently professor emerita. For her professional work, Dr. Bozeman has been recognized by many organizations, including Spelman College, the Mathematical Association of America (MAA), the National Association of Mathematicians (NAM), and the Quality Education for Minorities in Science and Engineering Network.

Her activities as a mentor were recognized by the Dr. Etta Z. Falconer Award for Mentoring and Commitment to Diversity at the Infinite Possibilities Conference in 2007, and by a Mentor Award from the American Association for the Advancement of Science (AAAS). She was elected the AAAS Fellow in 2010, and selected for the inaugural class of Fellows of the American Mathematical Society in 2013 and for the inaugural class of Association of Women in Mathematics (AWM) Fellows in 2018.

In retirement Dr. Bozeman continues to be professionally active through her membership on the EDGE Foundation Board, her work with several professional mathematics societies, and her membership on the President's Committee of the National Medal of Science. She enjoys traveling, playing English hand bells in her church hand bell choir, and serving in other church ministries. She is married to Robert E. Bozeman, a mathematician. They are the parents of two adult children and have two grandchildren. She is a member of Delta Sigma Theta Sorority, Inc.

Why is it important to encourage women to study math and science?

What is a mentor?

Fun with Magic Squares

There are different types of magic squares, and they are very fun to think about. For example, the square below becomes a magic square if you can use the numbers 1–9, only once each, to fill the square so that every row, column, and diagonal has a sum of 15. Try it!

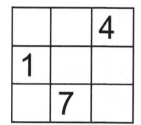 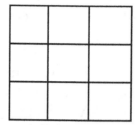

1. What patterns do you see in the magic square?
2. Can you mix the numbers up and find a new magic square for 15?
3. You can make any 3x3 magic square by using any nine consecutive numbers. Use the numbers 10–18 to fill in the magic square below. Hint: The sum of each row, column, and diagonal is 42.

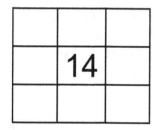

There are strategies to creating magic squares. If this is something that interests you, look it up and learn some useful strategies. For example, if you create an 8x8 magic square, you will need 64 boxes, therefore 64 numbers. If you use the numbers 1 to 64, so that each row, column, and diagonal adds up to the same number, it turns out that the number is the sum of the 64 consecutive numbers you use. In this case, $1 + 2 + 3 + \ldots + 63 + 64 = 260$. Therefore, the magic number for an 8x8 magic square that goes from 1 to 64 is 260. Try it!

4. Another type of magic square is one where every row, column, and diagonal has the same product! For example, the magic square below has a magic product of 1000. Complete the magic square using the nine divisors of 100.

5. Is there another number that has nine divisors that you can use in a 3x3 magic square? Draw your own magic square and try it!

Euler Graphs: Paths and Circuits

I.   An Euler (pronounced "oiler") path is a path that starts at one vertex and travels over each edge in a graph exactly once with no repeating over the same edge. It has a different starting and ending point.

For example: The path DABCDB is a path because it starts at Vertex D, ends at Vertex B, and travels over each edge only once with no repeats.

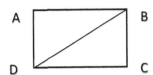

II. An Euler circuit is a path that travels over each edge in a graph exactly once with no repeating over the same edge. It has the same starting and ending point.

For example: The path ABCDA is a circuit. It starts and ends at Vertex A and travels over each edge exactly once with no repeats.

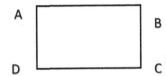

III. A graph is called an Euler graph if it has an Euler circuit. Tell whether each of these graphs has an Euler path, an Euler circuit, or neither. Write the path for each.

a.

b.

c.

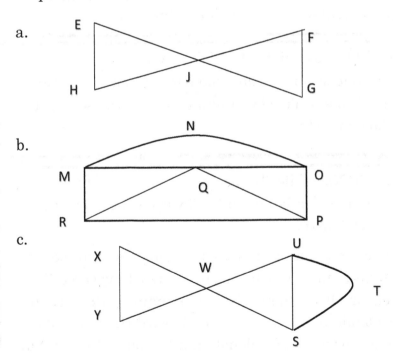

IV. Create/draw an Euler path that is not a circuit. Draw an Euler circuit.

Dr. Etta Zuber Falconer

"Dr. Falconer was my favorite professor. I love her so much".
Professor Kathaleena Edward Monds
Full Professor and Co-Director, Center for Economic Education/Small and
Minority Entrepreneurship, Albany State University

Etta Zuber was born in Tupelo, Mississippi, to Dr. Walter A. Zuber, a physician, and Mrs. Zadie L. Montgomery Zuber, a musician who had attended Spelman College. Etta attended public schools in Tupelo, graduating from the segregated George Washington High School in 1949.

She went on to Fisk University in Nashville, Tennessee, from which she graduated with high honors (summa cum laude) in 1953 with a bachelor's degree in mathematics and a minor in chemistry.

After Fisk, Etta earned a master of science degree in mathematics from the University of Wisconsin at Madison in 1954. She began her teaching career in 1954 at Okolona Junior College in Okolona, Mississippi, remaining there until 1963. During the 1963–64 academic year she taught at Howard High School in Chattanooga, Tennessee. While working at Okolona Junior College, Etta met and married her life partner of more than 35 years, Dolan P. Falconer.

Dr. Falconer's husband was soon offered and accepted a basketball coach position at Morris Brown College in Atlanta, Georgia. The family moved to Atlanta in 1965. It was then that Dr. Falconer began a 37-year career at Spelman College, also in Atlanta. She began as an instructor and was promoted to associate professor from 1965–71. During that time, she entered Emory University in Atlanta and earned a Ph.D. degree in mathematics in 1969. In later years, while at Spelman, she earned a master's degree in computer science from Atlanta University in 1982.

Dr. Falconer spent one year on the faculty at Norfolk State University in Norfolk, Virginia, but she returned to the faculty of Spelman College in 1972. Over her many years at Spelman College, she served in many positions including department chair, chair of the division of natural sciences, and director of science programs and policy. In 2002 Dr. Falconer retired from Spelman.

While at Spelman, Dr. Falconer positively impacted the lives of hundreds of Spelman students and faculty. She willingly shared her talents, time, and skills with African American women. She worked with several national mathematics societies including the American Mathematical Society (AMS), Association for Women in Mathematics (AWM), and Mathematical Association of America (MAA), to name a few. She was also a founder of the National Association of Mathematicians (NAM), an organization which promotes concerns of Black students and mathematicians.

For all her work, she received many awards and honors including Spelman's Presidential Award for Excellence in Teaching (1988) and Distinguished Service Award (1994), NAM's Distinguished Service Award (1994), AWM's Louise Hay Award (1995), and an honorary doctorate of science degree from the University of Wisconsin-Madison (1996). In 2001, Dr. Falconer won, along with Dr. James H.M.N. Henderson from Tuskegee University, the AAAS Lifetime Mentor Award. Her lifetime goal was to raise the number of African American women in mathematics and science. By many measures she accomplished her goal and has impacted women such as Dr. Kathaleena Monds, who recognizes Dr. Falconer as her favorite professor.

Dr. Falconer died in 2002 at the young age of 68. Survivors of Dr. Falconer include three children (Dolan P. Falconer, Jr., an engineer, Dr. Alice Falconer Wilson, a physician, and Dr. Walter Falconer, a physician) and ten grandchildren.

Color the historic **Sisters Chapel** at Spelman College in Atlanta, Georgia. Dr. Falconer and many of the students she mentored have spent many Sundays here. Also, Spelman faculty and staff, students' families, the community, and invited guests and scholars have also visited the chapel for various talks and events. As you color the beautiful Sisters Chapel, reflect on who you are now and who you wish to become.

Magic Squares Challenge

1. There are different types of magic squares, and they are very fun to think about. For example, the 4x4 square below becomes a magic square if you can complete it using the numbers from 1–16 only once so every row, column, and diagonal has the same sum. What is the magic sum?

16			
	11	10	
	7		
			1

2. Write the numbers 1 to 25 in the 5x5 magic square so that the sum of each row, column, and diagonal is 65. Look up the Siamese Method for help.

17				15
		13		
11				9

3. There are strategies to creating magic squares. If this is something that interests you, look it up and learn some useful strategies. For example, if you create an 8x8 magic square, you will need 64 boxes, therefore 64 numbers. If you use the numbers 1 to 64, so that each row, column, and diagonal adds up to the same number, it turns out that the number is the sum of the 64 consecutive numbers you use. In this case, $1 + 2 + 3 + ... + 63 + 64 = 260$. Therefore, the magic number for an 8x8 magic square that goes from 1 to 64 is 260. Try it!

Dr. Sadie Catherine Gasaway

Sadie Catherine Gasaway was born in Memphis, Tennessee, in 1914. She earned a bachelor's degree from LeMoyne College in Syracuse, New York, in 1941 and then earned a master's degree from the University of Illinois in 1945.

Mathematical Modeling at Work:

Which model represents $\frac{1}{2}$?

0   1

She earned her doctorate in 1961 from Cornell University in Ithaca, New York. Her dissertation was on consistent testing, which most schools now do every year. She is remembered because she was very involved in supporting students to continue exploring math. In that same year, she became a faculty member at Tennessee State University in Nashville.

Dr. Gasaway spent her entire career at Tennessee State as a professor, and in 1968 she was named chair of the department of physics and mathematics. She died at a young age from pneumonia in 1976. *Jet Magazine* listed Dr. Gasaway as a noted mathematics lecturer. The Sadie C. Gasaway Memorial Award has been given to a graduating student at Tennessee State University majoring in mathematics and excelling in scholarship.

Color By Number

Directions: Color all the ones in red. Color all the twos in yellow. Color all the threes in green. Color all the fours in blue. Color all the fives in orange. Color all the sixes in purple. What does the message say?

_____

Write about something that you like in math. For example, you could write about a positive experience you've had in math or a math game that you enjoy.

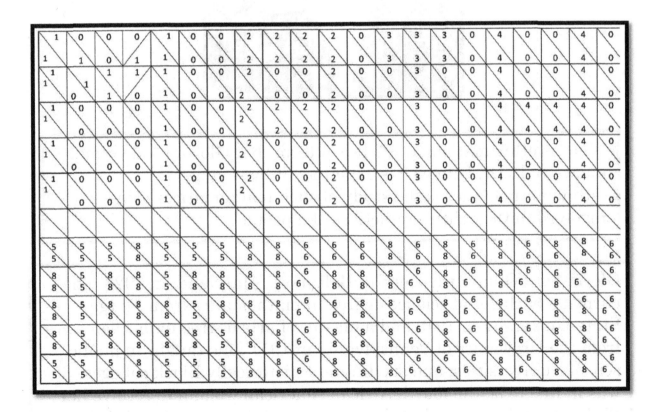

Dr. Gloria F. Gilmer

What is ethnomathematics? It is a term that Gloria Ford Gilmer knows well. Dr. Gilmer has explained it by saying, "ethnomathematics is the study of such mathematical ideas involved in the cultural practices of a people".

Gloria Ford Gilmer was born in Baltimore, Maryland, in 1928. She earned a bachelor of science degree in mathematics from Morgan State University in 1949 and a master of arts degree in mathematics from the University of Pennsylvania in 1951. She taught in public schools, universities, and six different historically Black colleges. She was in line to be the fourth African American woman to receive her Ph.D. in mathematics, but she took time off to raise a family. She later went back and received a Ph.D. in curriculum and instruction from Marquette University in Milwaukee, Wisconsin. She felt her enjoyment of mathematics outdid any disadvantages she had as a woman.

Dr. Gilmer was a leader in the field of ethnomathematics, the study of how different people in different cultures use mathematics. Even though all cultures use mathematics, they may use it in many different ways. One topic Dr. Gilmer especially enjoyed exploring was the different patterns that hairstylists create when braiding African American women's hair. She linked how these hair patterns (called tessellations) were often similar to the patterns found in nature. She especially enjoyed showing her students that mathematics can be found in many unexpected places.

Dr. Gilmer co-founded the International Study Group on Ethnomathematics (ISGE). She was a member of many mathematics associations and was even chosen to be a research associate for the United States Department of Education. She served as the president for Math Tech, Inc., a corporation that strives to blend educational research into effective ways to encourage women and minorities to explore mathematics.

Sometimes students feel that anything they learn in mathematics is useless. Dr. Gilmer worked hard to prove the opposite was true. She liked to encourage everyone to go out and find where mathematics is hidden in our everyday world.

In an interview Dr. Gilmer stated, "educators often overlook the importance of making emotional connections between students and the subject matter". Her article *Mathematical Patterns in African American Hairstyles* is an example of how she incorporates this principle.

Color Me Pretty!

Dr. Gilmer would see lots of math in this beautiful hairstyle.

What's That Word?

Directions: Solve each equation. Write the solution and then the corresponding letter. The letters will spell out the secret math word. Write the word on the line below and then define it.

1	2	3	4	5	6	7	8	9	10	11	12	13
A	B	C	D	E	F	G	H	I	J	K	L	M

14	15	16	17	18	19	20	21	22	23	24	25	26
N	O	P	Q	R	S	T	U	V	W	X	Y	Z

Equation	Solution	Solution's corresponding letter
$40 \div (3 + 5)$		
$\dfrac{60}{3}$		
$2 + 2 \times 3$		
$2 \times (3 + 4)$		
$\left(\dfrac{15}{3}\right) \times 3$		
$1 + 1 + 2 \times 5 + 1$		
12^0		
$2 \times 2 \times 10 \div 2$		
2^3		
$23^0 \times 10 \div 2$		
$\dfrac{69}{3} - 10$		
$7 \times 8 \div 56$		
$2 \times 2 \times 5$		
$(18 \div 6)^2$		
$\dfrac{27}{3^2}$		
$140 \div 7 - (8 - 7)$		

Secret word and definition: _____

Dr. Gloria Conyers Hewitt

"Gloria demanded work from the students and was willing to spend the amount of time needed to help them succeed. She was the type of professor that students should have".

Johnny W. Lott, professor emeritus
department of mathematical sciences,
The University of Montana, Missoula
past president, National Council of Teachers of Mathematics

Gloria Conyers Hewitt was born on October 26, 1935, in Sumter, South Carolina. Her parents Emmett and Crenella Conyers were both college graduates. In addition, all of her siblings attended college and earned graduate degrees.

Her parents made sacrifices to send her to Mather Academy, a coeducational boarding school in Camden, South Carolina, during segregation. After graduating high school, Gloria entered Fisk University in Nashville, Tennessee, in 1952. Fisk is a historically Black university and was formally called The Fisk Freed Colored School. It was at Fisk that Gloria realized she was interested in pursuing a career in mathematics.

She recalls going home for Christmas break and bringing only her calculus book home to work on word problems. It took her the full two weeks to work on just one problem because at that time she didn't really understand the process involved. After that, you could catch her sitting on campus doing calculus problems for fun! She was hooked on math!

At Fisk, Gloria worked under the tutelage of the department chair Lee Lorch, whose efforts for racial justice had an enormous impact on the lives of many Black mathematicians. After graduation, Dr. Lorch recommended Gloria for graduate school, and she accepted an offer to attend the University of Washington at Seattle. Gloria completed her bachelor of science degree in mathematics in 1956. When she attended graduate school she learned that her mathematics background was weak compared with that of the other students. She did not let that hinder her, and she was very fortunate to have considerable encouragement and help from her fellow graduate students, who mostly happened to be white males. She continued to work hard, and in 1960 she received her master of science degree in mathematics. Very shortly after, in the fall of 1961, she accepted a position as an assistant professor of mathematics at the University of Montana in Missoula, Montana. In 1962, Dr. Hewitt earned her Ph.D. in mathematics from the University of Washington.

Except for two year-long assignments at the National Science Foundation and at Case Western Reserve University, Dr. Hewitt has worked at the University of Montana continuously. She held several positions there including associate chair and chair of the department of mathematical sciences. She retired from the university in June 1999 and is currently professor emeritus in mathematics. One accomplishment that Dr. Hewitt is proud of is an article she wrote in 1979 that appeared in the *Annals of the New York Academy of Science*, entitled *The Status of Women in Mathematics*.

In addition to her university work, Dr. Hewitt has been a consultant to numerous academic institutions and an active participant in many professional organizations, including the Mathematical Association of America (MAA), American Mathematical Society (AMS), National Association of Mathematicians (NAM), and the Association for Women in Mathematics (AWM). Dr. Hewitt has been an important part of the mathematics community for over 50 years. She currently lives in Missoula, Montana.

Teaching Children is What I Love!

1. Color the math classroom and write about your favorite mathematics topic.
   _____

2. Is there a teacher, family member, or friend who inspires you to do mathematics? If so, how? _____

3. How can you inspire others? _____

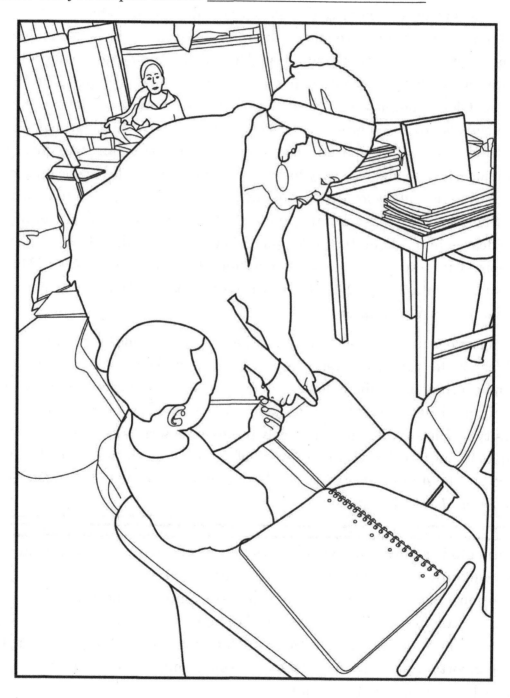

Lucky You!

Get smarter finding probability and statistics vocabulary!

```
            U Y B J K G W P          R A W A Q U U N
            E N X E K D B Z E E      J T M K F I M A G B
            O Z V R T Q C P G G Q    R A N D O M A V C U K
      S Y   J W G H Y E B R N U      U Y Y F B I N T A A   X M
    T H Y L   U T D R R S H A H      M S T H D S O R G   T N W L
    E G N P G J V J U T D I R D      N L F I I V N T F Y J A Z U
    A V Y Q I G V D Q A N K C X      Q Q L B L R J P H M E X D C
    C N B M K W A Y Q I Q Y J Q      U E M F I I I Z P L D N Y K
    B N P C S X Y T M N O R L C      A H M A U R B V Y P O A O Y
    A L G E G Q B M B Y O O T I      N L F H C G W A K R M E K N
    N C E Q F T Z N D Y Y G T E D    T P L A C A T G B Y K M I W
    Z E Q M X D P X B A C E Z C X I  S R C G K O K M O M P F Y
      Q U M A D K G I D F T K R O T  L G I Y U P H V V R K J
      Y H G G N G H P L A B E B A B  E R C Q U B L L U P
              W C G I Y T S U H
      F B I K O T B N L F S D G I H  G B S A D B J L A L
      G D F L E I K O A R G E R C V  V J E R A Q M E D I A N
    Q A P T L F E M O D C V D P U E  Q Z V N C I U B A E W R T
    C D B P E L B I S S O P M I H T  L U I V W I B R W F N O X
    H K M G P F Z E U V D G C E      T M O T G H R P I U C N C X
    W A K M A A C G T A O E J C      E X Z A F K V M D V Y J F Y
    S S G P J N C S Y C Q R I X      W I N T X A T Z R I S X J V
    V M D F A J S B V A G N C O      L I N I U F L F U M M A W M
    A O D H X O W Y A D Z D O L      Y K J L J H E N Z C P B G P
    G F C R   V E S O L Y L Q O      W O R A H X V I Y   K L Y E
      F H   S T A T I S T I C S      Q K S U Z B R C U I   Z A
            F U W U T K T K J C M    R H R Q L B Y C B S J
            H W O Y I J C J A H        E Q I A K V N C Y N
            R K F I Q P D K            A I M J V G A H
```

WORD LIST:

BIAS	GAME	MODE	SAMPLE
CATEGORY	IMPOSSIBLE	PROBABILITY	STATISTICS
CERTAIN	LOSE	QUALITATIVE	WIN
CHANCE	LUCKY	QUANTITATIVE	
DATA	MEAN	RANDOM	
FAIR	MEDIAN	RANGE	

Dr. Genevieve Madeline Knight

Dr. Knight was known to say that students should believe, "I can be anything I want to be if I prepare and work hard".

Genevieve Madeline Knight was born June 18, 1939, in Brunswick, Georgia. She grew up with two sisters, and each of them graduated as an honor student from Risley High School and Fort Valley State College (now known as Fort Valley State University). Dr. Knight remembers how close her family was growing up. Everyone in her family read and discussed issues of the day. They would sit around the table and exchange ideas. To show how close she and her sisters were, consider that in college all three sisters were members of Alpha Kappa Mu Honor Society, Beta Kappa Chi Scientific Honor Society, and Delta Sigma Theta Sorority.

Genevieve earned a bachelor of science degree in mathematics from Fort Valley State College in 1961 and a master of science degree in mathematics from Atlanta University in 1963. After Atlanta, Genevieve became a National Science Foundation (NSF) Fellow, taking advantage of institutes for college mathematics teachers. After getting her master's degree, she taught at Hampton Institute (now Hampton University) in Hampton, Virginia. Hampton is a historically Black college.

Dr. Knight was dedicated to teaching at historically Black colleges and universities (HBCUs), so after Hampton University she taught at Coppin State College in Baltimore, Maryland, from 1985 until she retired in 2006.

While at an NSF lecture, Genevieve was inspired by a woman who had a Ph.D. in mathematics. After meeting the woman, Genevieve decided that she would also like to get her doctorate degree. She went on to earn a Ph.D. in mathematics education from the University of Maryland in 1970. It's ironic that even though Dr. Knight has three degrees in mathematics, it was actually not her first choice of a college major.

Another person who inspired Dr. Knight was her thesis advisor at Atlanta University, Dr. Adulalim Shabazz. He introduced her to attending professional conferences and conventions, which became something she really enjoyed doing. One of the conferences she attended was the Annual Meeting of the National Council of Teachers of Mathematics (NCTM). In 1986 Dr. Knight and six other mathematics educators founded the Benjamin Banneker Association, Incorporated (BBA). The members of the BBA are dedicated to providing the highest quality mathematics education for African American students and all students. Over the years, Dr. Knight continued to be an advocate for equity for women and minorities in the mathematics and mathematics education communities. NCTM honored her with its Lifetime Achievement Award in 1999 for her 36 years of service to mathematics education.

She received many other awards over the years including distinguished teaching awards from both Hampton Institute and Coppin State College and the Dr. Etta Z. Falconer Award for Mentoring and Commitment to Diversity from the Infinite Possibilities Conference in 2015.

Dr. Genevieve Knight Maze

Follow Dr. Knight's achievements to get to the end of the maze here

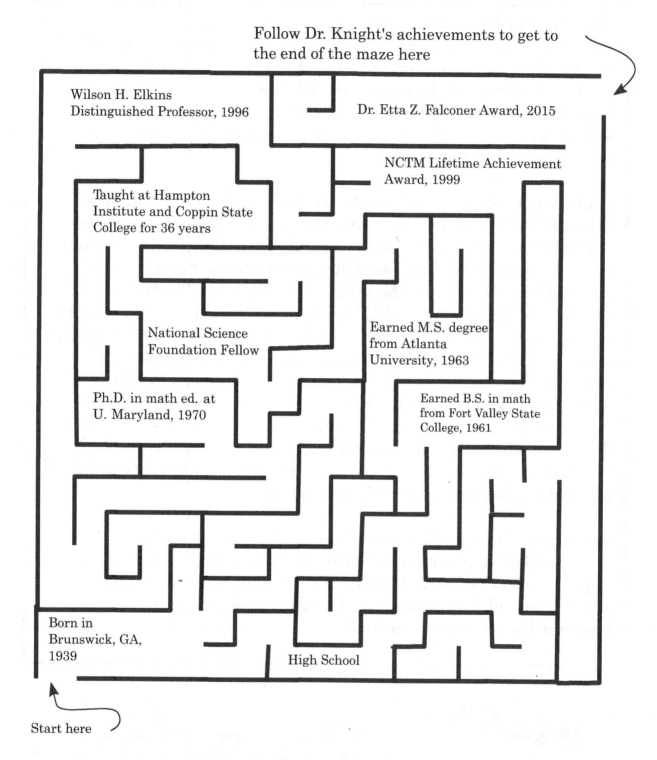

Wilson H. Elkins
Distinguished Professor, 1996

Dr. Etta Z. Falconer Award, 2015

NCTM Lifetime Achievement
Award, 1999

Taught at Hampton
Institute and Coppin State
College for 36 years

National Science
Foundation Fellow

Earned M.S. degree
from Atlanta
University, 1963

Ph.D. in math ed. at
U. Maryland, 1970

Earned B.S. in math
from Fort Valley State
College, 1961

Born in
Brunswick, GA,
1939

High School

Start here

Decode the Puzzle

Dr. Genevieve Knight was a founding member of this organization founded in 1986. This organization is an advocate for African American children with respect to the learning and teaching of mathematics.

Alphabet Chart

A	B	C	D	E	F	G	H	I	J	K	L	M
1	2	3	4	5	6	7	8	9	10	11	12	13

N	O	P	Q	R	S	T	U	V	W	X	Y	Z
14	15	16	17	18	19	20	21	22	23	24	25	26

Number Expression	Result	Letter from Alphabet Chart	Actual (Decoded) Letter
$5^2 \div 0.5 - 30 + 4$			
$1/3 \times 45 - 6$			
$(1200 - 7 \times 10^{10})/50$			
100^0			
0.08×75			
$(60 + 15) - (60 + 1)$			
$3^3 - 4$			
$7\frac{1}{2} \div 1\frac{1}{2}$			
$\sqrt{49}$			

Original Coded Message:

$\overline{}\ \overline{}\ \overline{}\ \overline{}\ \overline{}\ \overline{}\ \overline{}\ \overline{}\quad \overline{}\ \overline{}\ \overline{}\ \overline{}\ \overline{}\ \overline{}\ \overline{}\ \overline{}$
 24   1   10   6   23   9   5   10   24   23   10   10   1   7   1   14

Decoded Message—Name of Organization:

___ ___ ___ ___ ___ ___ ___ ___   ___ ___ ___ ___ ___ ___ ___ ___

Explain how you decoded the puzzle.

Dr. Carol E. Malloy

"All students have the ability to learn if given the opportunity".

Carol Flynn was born June 6, 1943, and raised in Harrisburg, Pennsylvania. In 1965 she earned a bachelor's degree in mathematics and education from West Chester University in West Chester, Pennsylvania, where she received a Distinguished Alumni Award in 2004. In 1970, she earned a master's degree in mathematics from Illinois Institute of Technology in Chicago. She spent more than 20 years as a middle- and high-school mathematics teacher in four urban school districts in Pennsylvania, Florida, and Wisconsin before joining the School of Education at UNC-Chapel Hill.

Dr. Malloy was a faculty member of the School of Education at UNC-Chapel Hill for 15 years. She joined the School of Education to serve as associate director of the Mathematics and Science Network. While serving in that role she earned a Ph.D. in curriculum and instruction from the school in 1994. She then joined the faculty, teaching secondary mathematics methods courses in the master of arts in teaching program, curriculum and foundations courses for graduate students, and mathematics for middle and elementary pre-service students. While at UNC-Chapel Hill Dr. Malloy received the University's Mentor Award for Lifetime Achievement (2009), the inaugural Impact Award from the Black Alumni of the School of Education (2010), and the School of Education's Distinguished Leadership Award. Dr. Malloy retired from the School of Education in 2009 but continued to work in mathematics education, serving as a lead author of mathematics textbooks.

One of Dr. Malloy's students, Dr. Robert Q. Berry, III, says that mathematics education scholars far and wide have looked to Dr. Malloy's work as seminal to the study of African American children in mathematics. In 2000, with fellow faculty member George Noblit and husband William Malloy, she co-authored *The Kids Got Smarter: Case Studies of Successful Comer Schools.* Throughout her career, Malloy worked to address the inequities that African American, Latino, and Native American students face in learning mathematics (NCTM website, May 15, 2013).

Throughout Dr. Malloy's four decades of work in mathematics education, she participated in many professional organizations including the National Council of Teachers of Mathematics (NCTM) and the Benjamin Banneker Association, Incorporated (BBA), where she served as president. She also served on the NCTM Board of Directors, edited yearbooks, reviewed journal manuscripts, wrote journal articles, served on committees, and gave countless presentations. In 2008, Dr. Malloy was selected to present NCTM's first annual Iris M. Carl Equity Address. For all of her hard work and dedication, Dr. Malloy received Lifetime Achievement Awards from both the NCTM and the BBA in 2013.

In Dr. Malloy's own words, she will be most remembered for being a supportive, caring, and demanding teacher: "I am a teacher. That's what I've done almost all my life. I teach". Malloy's son Michael Malloy said that he had learned a central lesson from his mother: "If you do not have a plan to succeed, you have a plan to fail".

Dr. Malloy died January 17, 2015, in Wilmington, North Carolina, where she lived with her husband William Malloy, also a retired School of Education faculty member.

Find the Treasure Chest

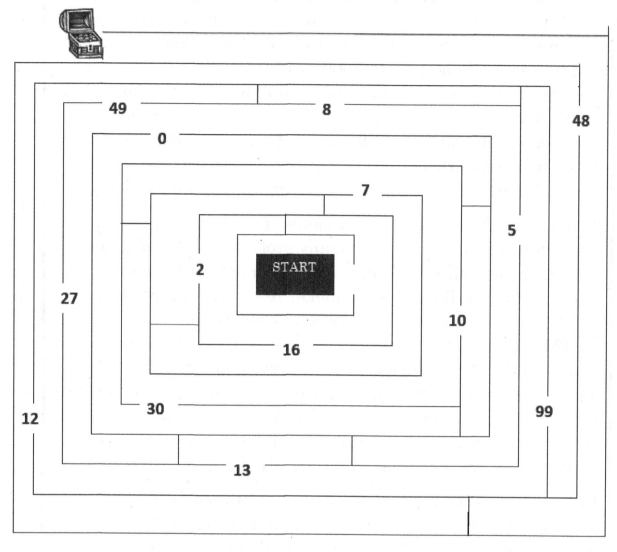

Help us find the treasure. Solve each problem. Each answer is a clue to which path to take.

a. $30 - 14 =$ _____   b. $21 \div 3 =$ _____   c. $5 \times 6 =$ _____

d. $0 \times 99 =$ _____   e. $(6 \times 6) + (6 + 7) =$ _____

f. $10^2 - 1 =$ _____   g. $46\frac{3}{4} + 1\frac{1}{4} =$ _____

Benjamin Banneker Gears

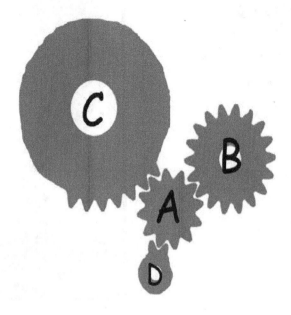

Carol Malloy was a lifetime member of the Benjamin Banneker Association, Incorporated (BBA), named after the astronomer, scientist, and mathematician Benjamin Banneker. The BBA is a national non-profit organization and affiliate partner of the National Council of Teachers of Mathematics (NCTM), dedicated to making sure that all children, particularly African American children, have access to the highest quality education that empowers them to gain the self confidence, enthusiasm, and endurance needed to succeed in mathematics and to transform themselves and their communities.

In 1753 Benjamin Banneker built a striking wooden clock which kept accurate time for 53 years. This is known to be the first clock made entirely in the United States. Calculating the proper number of teeth for each gear and the necessary relationships between the gears is an important part of making this clock.

Banneker clocks have gears that make the hands on the clocks rotate. There are missing teeth on gears C and D. For every full rotation gear C makes, gear A makes three rotations. Gear D rotates twice for every rotation gear A makes. Gear A has 12 teeth.

1. How many teeth does gear C have? _____
   How many teeth does gear D have? _____
2. If gear C makes two full rotations, how many full rotations does gear B make? _____
   How many full rotations does gear D make? _____

Dr. Vivienne Lucille Malone-Mayes

Vivienne Lucille Malone was born on February 10, 1932, in Waco, Texas. Her parents Pizarro and Vera Estelle Allen Malone were both teachers. She attended segregated schools while she was growing up and graduated from the segregated A. J. Moore High School in 1948 in Waco.

Segregated schools meant that the Black and white children were not allowed to attend the same schools. She enjoyed school, and she first became aware what segregation meant when she was a small child and drank from a "whites only" drinking fountain. She later learned which playgrounds she could play on and which stores she could shop in. She is known because she was the first African American to be a full-time professor at Baylor University.

Vivienne Malone went to Fisk University when she was only 16 years old. While she was there, she became friends with Gloria Conyers Hewitt and Etta Zuber Falconer, both of whom later earned Ph.D.s in mathematics. She earned a bachelor's degree in 1952 and a master's degree two years later from Fisk.

While at Fisk, she took courses from Dr. Evelyn Boyd Granville (also featured in this book). After graduating from Fisk, Malone chaired the mathematics departments at two historically Black colleges: Paul Quinn and Bishop Colleges. In 1961, she decided to take additional classes at Baylor University. Even though she had two degrees in mathematics, Baylor refused to accept her because it was still segregated. Instead, she attended the University of Texas (UT) at Austin. During the time she was there she was the only African American and the only woman enrolled. Even though UT-Austin was desegregated she still faced racism and sexism. In fact, one professor refused to teach her, and many of the other students ignored her. She felt alone and couldn't even attend off-campus meetings because the coffee shop where they were held could not serve Blacks, according to Texas law. To combat the racism, she participated in many civil rights demonstrations and picket lines. The reason behind the demonstrations was to force the integration of restaurants and movie houses. In 1966, she received a Ph.D. in mathematics from UT-Austin.

By the time she earned her Ph.D., Baylor University had desegregated, and Dr. Malone-Mayes was hired as the first African American faculty member there. For the 25 years she taught there, she enjoyed working at the university and encouraging her students. The Student Congress even elected her the "Outstanding Faculty Member of the Year" in 1971. She retired in 1994 because she was ill.

In addition to her position at Baylor, Dr. Malone-Mayes was active in professional organizations. She was the first African American elected to the Executive Committee of the Association for Women in Mathematics (AWM). She was a member of the Board of Directors of the National Association of Mathematicians (NAM) and was elected director-at-large for the Texas section of the Mathematical Association of America (MAA).

Dr. Malone-Mayes was also active in her community and church and served on numerous organizations' Boards of Directors. She has a daughter, Patsyanne Mayes Wheeler.

Dr. Vivienne Malone-Mayes died in 1995 at the young age of 63.

Tangram Coloring

The tangram puzzle consists of seven geometric pieces which are normally boxed in the shape of a square. The pieces, called "tans", are used to create different patterns such as a man and his dog. Color the tangram picture.

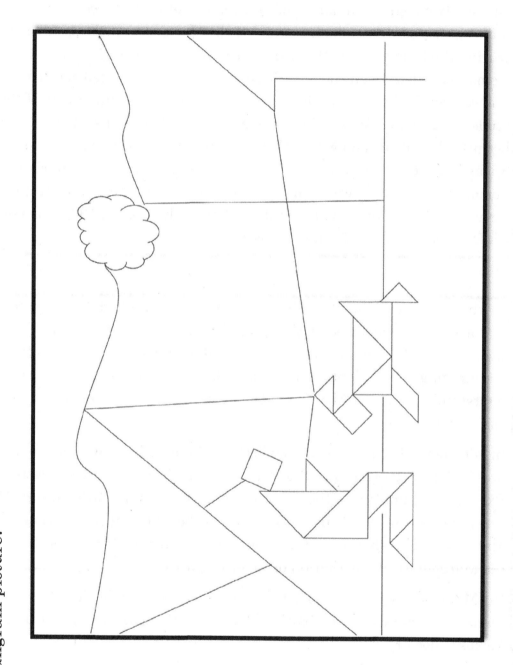

44

Making Tangram Figures

Cut out the seven tangram shapes in the large square below. What other cool figures can you make using all seven pieces? Can you make a duck? A flower? What else? Now that you've cut out the seven shapes, can you recreate the large tangram square?

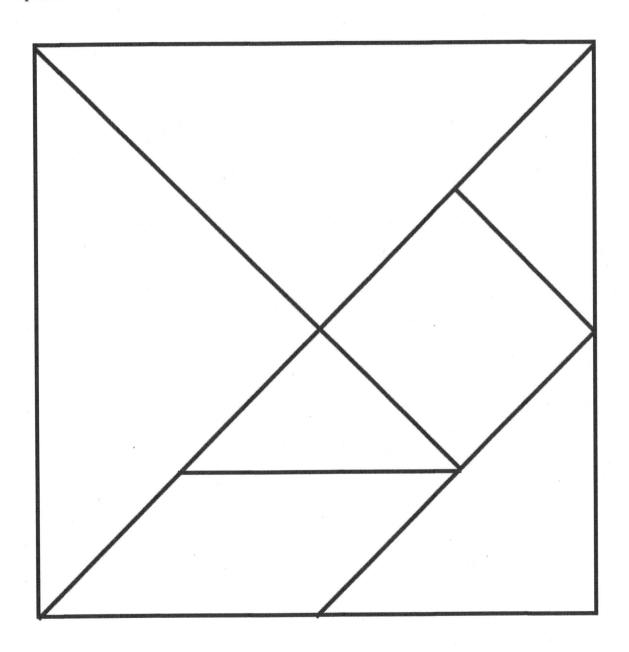

Mystery Shape Equations

Solve the equations to find the values of the mystery shapes.

□ + ○ + □ + ⬯ = 25

⬯ + ⬯ + ⬯ + □ = 14

○ − □ = 7

□ = _____

○ = _____

⬯ = _____

47

Dr. Argelia Velez-Rodriguez

Argelia Velez was born in Havana, Cuba, in 1936. She attended Roman Catholic primary and secondary schools where she showed ability in mathematics at an early age. Argelia's father, Pedro Velez, was in the Cuban Congress, and at that time Fulgencio Batista was the President of Cuba. Around 1952, Velez was studying mathematics at the Marianao Institute. Even though Velez did not suffer racial or gender discrimination in Cuba, the country was still experiencing bad times under President Batista, who had retired but was returned to power by an army revolt.

In 1954, Velez married Raul Rodriguez while she was an undergraduate student in college. Their first child, a son, was born in 1955. After earning a bachelor's degree from the Marianao Institute in 1955, Velez-Rodriguez continued on to graduate studies at the University of Havana, majoring in both astronomy and mathematics. Astronomy is the study of stars, planets, space, and other non-Earthly bodies and phenomena.

At the University of Havana, most of her teachers were women and most had doctorate degrees, so it was perfectly natural for a woman in Cuba to be undertaking doctoral studies in mathematics.

Cuban Street Scene

Velez-Rodriguez earned a Ph.D. in mathematics from the University of Havana in 1960. She became the first Black woman to receive a doctorate in mathematics at the University of Havana. During her doctoral studies the couple's second child, a daughter, was born in 1959.

After her daughter was born, Velez-Rodriguez became increasingly unhappy with communism in Cuba. She decided to go to the United States so that her children could have a better education. She emigrated from Cuba to the United States in 1962. At the time, her husband was unable to leave Cuba with her, but after three years he was able to join her in the United States. Although life was in many ways much better in the United States than it had been in Cuba, Dr. Velez-Rodriguez experienced racial and gender discrimination for the first time.

In 1962 Velez-Rodriguez began teaching mathematics and physics at Texas College. It was in 1970 that she first became involved with the science education programs of the National Science Foundation, and this marks the start of what would eventually become her life's work. She taught at several historically Black colleges before joining Bishop College in Dallas, Texas, in 1972. Seeing minority students at a disadvantage because of racism, Velez-Rodriguez experimented with different ways of teaching mathematics that would be particularly beneficial to minority and disadvantaged students. She wanted to encourage them to pursue careers in mathematics and science. In 1972, Velez-Rodriguez became an American citizen. She was appointed chair of the department of mathematical science at Bishop College from 1975 to 1978.

In 1979, she became a program manager with the Minority Institutions Science Improvement Program in Washington, DC, and then the director of the Minority Science Improvement Program at the US Department of Education.

Her move to the United States to give her children a good education paid off. Her son became a surgeon, and her daughter became an engineer and earned a master's degree in business administration (M.B.A.) from Harvard University in Cambridge, Massachusetts.

Argelia Velez-Rodriguez was born in Havana, Cuba. Color the Cuban street scene and then do further research on the country. What have you found that is interesting about Cuba?

Fraction Facts:
Color the Planets

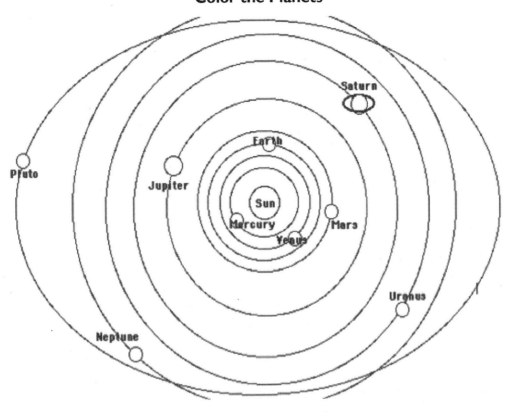

Perform the operations below. Match the numerator answer with the planet in the table and denominator answer with the color code. Then color the planets above. Do not simplify.

Ex: $\frac{1}{2} + \frac{2}{2} = \frac{3}{2}$ The numerator is 3, which matches with Earth. The denominator is 2, which matches with light blue, so you would color the Earth light blue.

$$\frac{1}{4} + \frac{5}{4} =$$ $$\frac{3}{7} + \frac{2}{7} =$$ $$\frac{1}{3} + \frac{1}{3} =$$

$$\frac{8}{9} - \frac{1}{9} =$$ $$\frac{9}{10} - \frac{5}{10} =$$ $$\frac{12}{13} - \frac{11}{13} =$$

$$\frac{5}{7} \times \frac{3}{2} =$$ $$\frac{10}{11} \times \frac{5}{3} =$$ $$\frac{1}{3} \times \frac{20}{13} =$$

Coloring Codes

Numerator	Pluto (4)	Uranus (15)	Sun (7)	Venus (6)	Mars (20)	Saturn (5)	Mercury (2)	Jupiter (50)	Neptune (1)	Earth (3)
Denominator	Light Blue (2)	Red (39)	Orange (33)	Pale Yellow (4)	Brown (10)	Grey (3)	Green (14)	Dark Blue (13)	Yellow (9)	Pale Gold (7)

51

Chapter 3: The Un-Hidden Figures

Dr. Christine Mann Darden

> "All things work together for the good of those that love the Lord and are called according to his purpose"

Christine Mann was born on September 10, 1942, in Monroe, North Carolina, to Noah Horace Sr., an insurance agent, and Desma Chaney Mann, an elementary school teacher. Being the youngest of five children, Christine's mother took her to school with her at the age of three. While Christine's mother taught the other children, Christine learned, too. At home, Christine continued to learn by taking apart and reconstructing bicycles and helping her dad fix cars on the weekends. Christine started high school at Winchester Avenue High School but then transferred to Allen High School (formerly the Allen School for Negro Girls), a Methodist boarding school in Asheville, North Carolina. She graduated from Allen High School in 1958 as the class valedictorian and received a scholarship to attend Hampton Institute in Hampton, Virginia (now Hampton University).

While Christine was in college, she took part in the civil rights protests and sit-ins with other students, and she also worked the voter registration drives to get fellow Hampton students and Black neighbors in Hampton to register and vote in the presidential election that year. In 1962, she received her bachelor of science degree in mathematics and a teaching certificate from Hampton Institute.

From 1962–1965 Christine taught high school mathematics. It was during that time in 1963 that she met and married Walter L. Darden Jr., a science teacher. After marrying Darden, she became a research assistant in aerosol physics at Virginia State College, and then went on to earn her master of science degree in applied mathematics from Virginia State College in 1967 (now Virginia State University).

That same year, she learned that the National Aeronautics and Space Administration (NASA) was recruiting. She applied for a position at NASA and was hired as a data analyst assigned to the pool of human computers. At NASA's Langley Research Center, "she wrote complex programs and tediously crunched numbers for the engineers" (NASA, 2013). Dr. Darden said that it wasn't until she got to NASA that she learned how close her applied mathematics was to what theoretical engineers did. She fought to become an engineer as she saw men with her same credentials promoted before her. In 1973, she was promoted to the position of aerospace engineer. As an engineer, Darden was approved for educational leave. She continued her education at George Washington University and, in 1983, earned a doctorate degree in mechanical engineering.

In 1989, Dr. Darden was appointed as the technical leader of NASA's Sonic Boom Group Program. She had other promotions while at NASA and was the first African American woman at NASA Langley to be promoted into the senior executive service. She is also the author of more than 50 publications at NASA and has been given many awards including ten Certificates of Outstanding Performance from NASA. "Christine Darden's 40-year career at NASA led her to become one of the world's experts on sonic boom prediction, sonic boom minimization and supersonic wing design" (NASA, 2013). Outside of NASA she also received the Dr. A. T. Weathers Technical Achievement Award from the National Technical Association in 1985, the 1987 Candace Award for Science and Technology from the National Coalition of 100 Black Women, the 1988 Black Engineer of the Year Award from the publishers of *US Black Engineer and Information Technology Magazine,* and the Senior Executive Career Development Fellowship from Simmons College in 1994.

Christine Darden and her husband raised three children. When her children were small, Darden was a Girl Scout mom. She also sang in the church choir and was a Sunday school teacher. Dr. Darden is a grandmother of five and a great-grandmother of three. Her favorite color is green and her favorite season is fall. Dr. Darden seems to like nature, so it is no surprise that she likes to vacation in the mountains.

Dr. Christine Darden

Complete the crossword puzzle below. Use the History Makers website for more information on Dr. Darden.

Across

2. Darden's first job at NASA was a _____ analyst
5. Christine Darden was born in this state
7. Christine Darden's favorite season is ____
8. Christine is one of _____ children
9. Darden's first job was a _____ teacher
10. Christine has received many _____ and medals for her accomplishments
11. Darden has been published more than ____ times!
13. Christine's favorite color is _____

Down

1. Christine Darden received a degree in math education from ____ Institute
3. In 1973, Christine was promoted by NASA to an _____ engineer
4. A student who has the highest rank in their graduating class
6. Christine's mom was a _____
12. Christine received the Certificate of Outstanding Performance from NASA ____ times

Tessellation Darden

To create a tessellation: Color the airplanes. Try to use no more than three colors. Then, cut out the airplanes and try to fit them together in a pattern. You should have no overlaps or gaps between each shape. You can flip (reflect), turn (rotate), or slide (translate) the shapes. When you are happy with your design, glue them on a blank piece of paper.

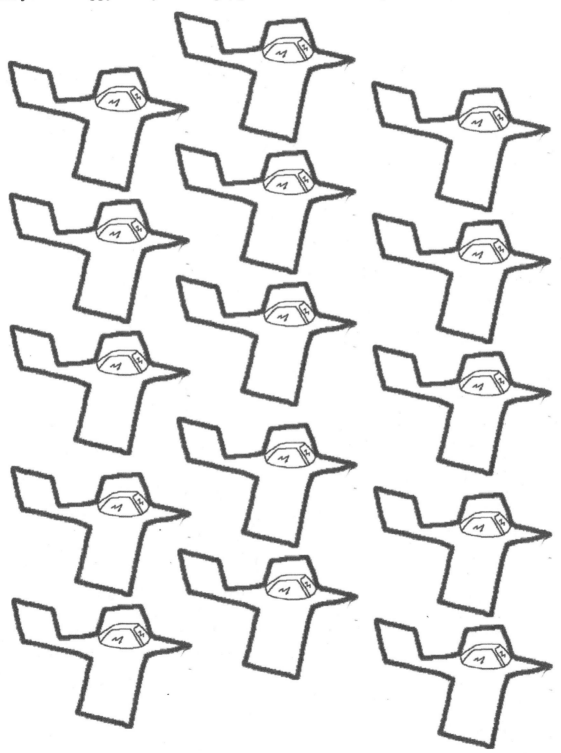

Sudoku Puzzle Fun

A sudoku puzzle is a grid of 9x9 squares subdivided into nine 3x3 squares. To solve the puzzle, enter the digits 1–9 into each 3x3 grid. You may use each digit, 1–9, ONLY once in each 3x3 grid. Each column and row of the large 9x9 grid also has each digit, 1–9, ONLY once. Can you do it? Is there more than one solution?

2	8		6	9	7		4	3
1			8	2	5		7	9
		6				5	2	8
	2	7	3		9		8	
6					8	7		5
4		8	7		1	3	6	
		9			6	2	3	
	5	2	4	8				6
3		1				8	5	4

Mary Winston Jackson

Mary Winston was born on April 9, 1921, in Hampton, Virginia. She graduated with high honors from Phenix High School located on the Hampton Institute campus. Mary graduated college from the Hampton Institute (now Hampton University) in 1942. At a time when most of Hampton Institute's female students earned degrees in home economics or nursing, Mary earned two bachelor's degrees, one in mathematics and the other in physical science. Mary's parents, Frank Winston and Ella Scott Winston, were also graduates of the Hampton Institute. Mary pledged the Alpha Kappa Alpha Sorority, Incorporated, as an undergraduate at the Hampton Institute.

After graduating from the Hampton Institute, Ms. Winston taught mathematics at a Negro high school in Maryland for one year. In 1943, she became a secretary and bookkeeper for the United Service Organizations (USO). While working at the USO, Mary met and married Levi Jackson, who worked as a painter at the Langley Field in Hampton, Virginia. Langley Field, founded in 1916, was the home of a pioneering military air strip. In 1946 Levi and Mary welcomed their first child, Levi Jr. When Levi was a young boy his mother helped him design a soapbox car, which he raced in the town's annual derby race and won. He was the first colored boy in the history of their town to win the soapbox derby. Mary recognized that "being part of a Black First was a powerful symbol" (Shetterly, 2016, p. 200). The Jacksons had two children, son Levi Jr. and daughter Carolyn. Mary was a pillar in her community, being a devout member of the African Methodist Episcopal Church and a longtime Girl Scout leader. Mary went out of her way to encourage students in her community to consider science and engineering as career choices. She started an after-school science club for students and also tutored students in mathematics and science.

3.141592 6

In 1951 Mary was hired at the National Advisory Committee for Aeronautics (NACA) as a computer. They referred to the women mathematicians as "computers" at NACA's Langley Memorial Aeronautical Laboratory located in Hampton, Virginia. Her official title was research mathematician, and she worked under Dorothy Vaughan (also featured in this book). During her years at NACA, Mary worked in the Supersonic Pressure Tunnel and eventually moved to the Compressibility Research Division. She was assigned to work with the flight engineers at NASA who were all men. NACA became NASA in 1958. Mary desired to be an engineer, but first she had to get special permission to take several additional courses at a segregated high school in town. Once approved, Mary joined a special training program and was promoted to aerospace engineer. She became NASA's first Black female engineer. Mrs. Jackson authored or co-authored 12 technical papers for NACA and NASA. In a 1977 interview, Mary Jackson told *Ebony Magazine*, "I've always liked math", and that is what brought her to NASA (the National Aeronautics and Space Administration).

After 34 years at NASA, Mrs. Jackson reached the highest level of engineer that was possible for her without becoming a supervisor. She decided to change positions in order to challenge discrimination in the workplace and help women of color to advance their careers. She went to NASA headquarters in Washington, DC, to train to become an equal opportunity specialist. In her new position, she advised women and minorities how to get further training so that they could change their titles from mathematicians to engineers to increase their chances of promotion. She worked at NASA until her retirement in 1985.

Mary Winston Jackson died on February 11, 2005.

The story of Mary W. Jackson's life at NACA/NASA is depicted in the 2016 film *Hidden Figures* about three African American women mathematicians who contributed to the 1960s space race.

5 3 5 8 9 7 9 3 2 3...

Brain Buster

Paola, Sonia, Isabelle, Owen, and Teddy raced to the park. Use the clues below to find which friend arrived at the park in third place.

Sonia did not finish last.

Teddy arrived before Owen.

One person finished before Teddy.

Isabelle arrived after Owen.

Paola came in second to last.

_____ _____ _____ _____ _____
First   Second   Third   Fourth   Fifth

Wind Tunnel Math

Directions: Each face has a number, and each is separated by an operation: +, −, *, ÷. Connect the faces of Mary Winston Jackson on the wind tunnel to make the largest number possible. You may only use each number once, and you must follow a path. For example, 5 − 4 = 1. Then 1 − 1 = 0. Then 0 + 2 = 2. Finally 2 * 3 = 6. (The path would be written as 5 − 4 − 1 + 2 * 3. Note: These are "paths"; therefore, we are NOT using order of operations. There are many possible paths. Have fun!)

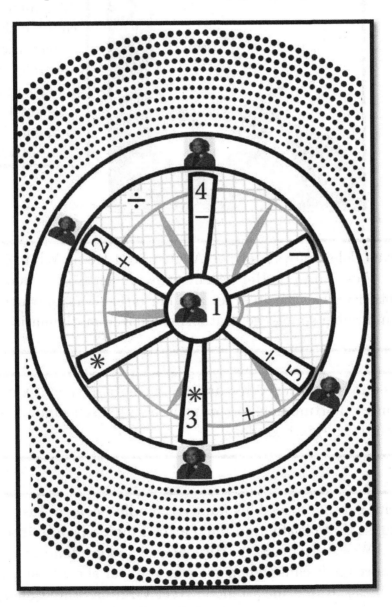

The greatest path is _____ = ____

Katherine Coleman Goble Johnson

"I counted everything. I counted the steps to the road, the steps up to church, the number of dishes and silverware I washed … anything that could be counted, I did" (NASA, 2015).

Katherine Coleman was born on August 26, 1918, in White Sulphur Springs, West Virginia. Her parents were Joylette and Joshua Coleman. Her mother was a schoolteacher and her father was a farmer and bellman. From a young age, Katherine enjoyed mathematics.

She loved to count everything and could easily solve mathematical equations. Unfortunately, in her hometown the school for Negro children only went to the sixth grade.

Katherine's father moved his family 125 miles away to Institute, West Virginia, so that his children could attend high school. Katherine attended West Virginia State High School and graduated at the young age of fourteen, because when she was younger she was skipped two grades ahead. Katherine attended West Virginia State College (now West Virginia State University) with a full academic scholarship because she had excellent grades. In 1937 at only 18 years old, Katherine received bachelor of science degrees in French and mathematics.

Katherine Coleman's first teaching job was at the high school in Marion, Virginia, from 1937 to 1939. She met her husband James F. Goble there. He was a chemistry teacher and she was a mathematics teacher.

In 1939, West Virginia integrated its graduate schools, and Katherine was one of the first three Negro students selected to desegregate the graduate program at West Virginia State College. After the first session, however, she decided to leave school and start a family with her husband James. They had three daughters: Joylette, Constance (Connie), and Kathy. When the girls got older, Katherine returned to teaching until she heard about a government facility in Hampton, Virginia, hiring Black women mathematicians.

Katherine and her husband moved their family to Hampton, Virginia, and she was hired by the National Advisory Committee for Aeronautics (NACA). In 1953, she joined NACA's Langley Memorial Aeronautical Laboratory as a research mathematician. She started in the segregated West Computing section under the supervision of Dorothy Vaughan. The pool of women mathematicians performing data reduction calculations were known as "computers". Just two weeks into Katherine's tenure at Langley, Dorothy Vaughan assigned her to a project in the Flight Research Division, where her position soon became permanent. She spent the next four years analyzing data from flight tests, and worked on the investigation of a plane crash caused by an encounter with wake turbulence. She was assertive, asking to be included in the all-male editorial meetings. It was during this time that her husband James died in December 1956.

Upon leaving the Flight Mechanics Branch, Katherine went on to join the Spacecraft Controls Branch where she calculated the flight trajectory for Alan Shepard, the first American to go into space in 1959.

In that same year, Katherine experienced a highlight of her life. She met Colonel James A. Johnson at church, and after a short courtship they were married. Katherine's job became very intense during this time and she spent many hours at work. Amazingly, Katherine found time to spend with her family, sing in the church choir, and work on service projects with her sorority sisters of Alpha Kappa Alpha Sorority, Incorporated.

Katherine Johnson is most known for verifying the mathematics behind Astronaut John Glenn's orbit around the Earth in 1962. She is also known for calculating the flight trajectory for Apollo 11's flight to the moon in 1969.

Mrs. Johnson retired from NASA in 1986. She has received many honors and awards for her important work with NASA. She has received honorary degrees from the State University of New York, Capitol College, Old Dominion University, and Spelman College. In 2015, President Barack Obama awarded her the Presidential Award of Freedom for being a pioneer of African American women in STEM fields.

Katherine Johnson resides in Virginia. She has two daughters: Joylette Hylick and Katherine Moore. A third daughter, Constance, is deceased.

Katherine Johnson Riddle

Why wasn't Katherine Johnson upset she didn't get to go to the moon?

Solve the following problems to find the answer to the riddle. Circle the correct answers in the chart, then solve the riddle.

1. $R + 10 = 4$
2. $M - 5 = -2$
3. $9 \times O = -36$
4. $\dfrac{T}{5} = 14$
5. $-4 + E = -16$
6. $-88 = -8D$
7. $I - (-3) = 19$
8. $C + 11 = 80$
9. $-24 + P = -3$
10. $70 = 2A$
11. $25U = -75$
12. $H + 7 = 15$
13. $\dfrac{G}{16} = -1$

R	6	-6	14	-14
M	-3	7	3	-7
O	4	3	-5	-4
T	2.5	70	12	19
E	-20	-12	20	12
D	-11	-80	11	80
I	16	22	-22	-16
C	-69	7.5	59	69
P	-21	21	8	-8
A	-35	35	68	72
U	3	50	-3	100
H	22	-8	-22	8
G	-16	16	1	-1

16		69	-4	3	21	-3	70	-12	11

70	8	-12		21	35	70	8			70	-4

-16	-12	70		70	8	-12	-6	-12

66

Katherine Johnson Word Search

Find the words that describe the life of Mrs. Katherine Johnson.

```
                Y  A
                L  W
             N  T  X  G
             X  Y  D  O
          R  O  F  D  I  E
          J  V  M  N  P  S
    T  N  B  V  I  R  G  I  N  I  A  C  P  U  N  F  X  S  Q  G
    G  M  W  T  V  E  G  H  I  Q  I  Y  M  A  X  Z  P  L  K  S
       F  I  G  U  R  E  S  W  T  R  G  I  A  U  G  U  S  T
          H  Z  Y  G  W  D  U  O  P  C  O  U  N  T  E  M
             A  P  P  W  A  T  C  I  D  O  U  R  M  O
                P  R  N  C  D  T  O  S  V  A  T  D
             Z  U  O  E  A  A  N  E  M  S  L  E  K  N
             Q  R  J  L  M  O  Z  A  C  P  E  S  P  E
       E  E  A  E  E  L  J  K  U  S  R  U  M  P  V  I
       A  R  D  H  L  Q  O        F  A  H  T  E  A  P
    K  T  D  T  P  K  M           K  E  L  E  D  C  Q
    L  Y  A  G  V                 O  L  R  A  E
 G  J  M  F                       L  J  L  Y
 N  Q                             C  A
```

AERONAUTICS
APOLLO
AUGUST
COMPUTER
COUNT
FIGURES
FREEDOM
MATHEMATICIAN
MEDAL
NASA
OF
SPACE
TRAJECTORY
VIRGINIA

Dorothy Johnson Vaughan

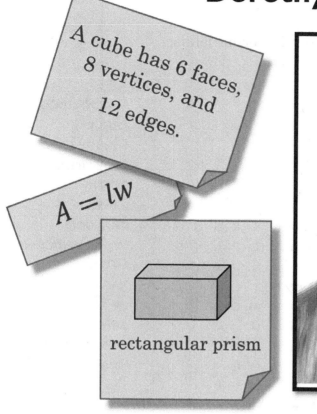

A cube has 6 faces, 8 vertices, and 12 edges.

$A = lw$

rectangular prism

Dorothy Johnson was born on September 10, 1910, in Kansas City, Missouri. Her mother, Annie A. Johnson, died when she was just two years old; therefore, Dorothy was raised by her father, Leonard Johnson, and her stepmother, Susie Peeler Johnson. Her family moved to Morgantown, West Virginia, in 1917 and Dorothy attended Beechurst High School. In 1925, she graduated high school as valedictorian at the age of 15, because she had been put ahead two grades (Shetterly, 2016). She attended Wilberforce University in Xenia, Ohio, on a full-tuition scholarship. Wilberforce University is the nation's oldest private, historically Black university. She became a member of the Alpha Kappa Alpha Sorority, Incorporated, in 1926.

Dorothy graduated with a bachelor's degree in mathematics in 1929. After graduation, she worked as a mathematics and English teacher, first in Illinois for one year and then for a brief period in North Carolina. Unfortunately, both of these Black segregated schools were shut down because of lack of funds. Dorothy got another teaching job at Robert Russa Moton High School in Farmville, Virginia. Ms. Johnson believed that education was necessary to protect Black people from the unjust world of the Jim Crow south. The Jim Crow laws in the south were state and local laws that enforced racial segregation.

Years after Ms. Johnson left the Russa Moton school, it became a National Historic Landmark and museum—it is known for being the student birthplace of America's Civil Rights Revolution. In 1951, the students at the school walked out and led a strike to protest the horrible conditions at the school. This student-led protest along with others helped the Supreme Court's 1954 Brown v. Board of Education decision that declared the practice of racially segregated schools unconstitutional.

Dorothy married Howard Vaughan and they had six children: Ann, Maida, Leonard, Kenneth, Donald, and Michael. Mrs. Vaughan applied for a mathematics job that would pay more than twice her teacher's salary and ensure that her children could attend college (Shetterly, 2016). She was hired at the National Advisory Committee for Aeronautics (NACA) and was assigned to the West Area Computers, a segregated group of Black women who worked on mathematical calculations for the engineers conducting aeronautical experiments.

In 1949, Dorothy Vaughan was promoted to head the group, making her the NACA's first Black supervisor and one of the NACA's few female supervisors. It took years in the role, however, before she gained the "official" title of supervisor. She was the supervisor for the West Area Computers until 1958, when the NACA became the National Aeronautics and Space Administration (NASA) and segregated facilities and work units were abolished. She then joined the new Analysis and Computation Division (ACD), a racially and gender-integrated group on the frontier of electronic computing. As a member of the Numerical Techniques Branch, she became an expert FORTRAN programmer and contributed to the Scout Launch Vehicle Program. Mrs. Vaughan had a 28-year career at Langley from 1943–1971 and retired at the age of 60. She lived in Newport News, Virginia, and was a 50-year member of the St. Paul AME Church where she participated in music and missionary activities.

Dorothy Vaughan died on November 10, 2008, in Hampton, Virginia, at the age of 98. She was preceded in death by her husband Howard S. Vaughan Jr. and two sons Michael J. and Donald H. Vaughan.

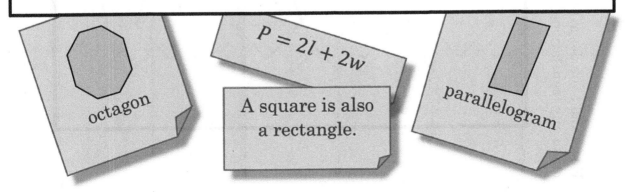

octagon

$P = 2l + 2w$

A square is also a rectangle.

parallelogram

Color the Fish Tessellation

How would you describe your design to a friend? Can you talk about any of the fish transformations? Does the fish make any translations (slides), rotations (turns), or reflections (flips)?

Decode the Message about Dorothy Vaughan

1. Solve the problems in Row 1. Write your answers in the blanks in Row 2.
2. Now solve the problems in Row 2. Record your final answers in Row 3.
3. Match the numbers in the boxes in Row 3 to the letters below to find the answer to the puzzle.
4. Write the answer to the puzzle in Row 4. What did you find out about Dorothy Vaughan?

Row 1	27÷9	6x6	54÷9	14÷2	18÷6	24÷3	2x5	24÷2	20÷5	5x6	2x4	24÷6	35÷5
Row 2	= ___ ___ x8 = ___	= ___ ___ ÷12 = ___	= ___ ___ x6 = ___	= ___ ___ x6 = ___	= ___ ___ x5 = ___	= ___ ___ x9 = ___	= ___ ___ x6 = ___	= ___ ___ x3 = ___	= ___ ___ x4 = ___	= ___ ___ ÷10 = ___	= ___ ___ x7 = ___	= ___ ___ x8 = ___	= ___ ___ x3 = ___
Row 3													
Row 4													

A	B	C	D	E	F	G	H	I	J	K	L	M	N	O	P	Q	R	S	T	U	V	W	X	Y	Z
42	12	72	5	32	18	50	24	8	14	28	81	36	15	60	16	63	21	54	56	3	6	49	27	9	30

71

Quadrilateral Transformations

1. Number the x- and y-axes. Plot the ordered pairs on the grid below and then connect the points to create a quadrilateral. (4, 13); (11, 8); (7, 13); (4, 8)
2. Name the quadrilateral. _____
3. Double the x- and y-coordinates and plot the new points on the same grid below.

   (____,____)   (____,____)   (____,____)   (____,____)

4. What happened to the size of the quadrilateral after you doubled the coordinates?
5. What is the area of the original quadrilateral? _____
6. What is the area of the enlarged quadrilateral? _____
7. What does this tell you?
8. Double the x-coordinates only. Keep the y-coordinates the same. Plot the new points. Hint: Use a different color pen or pencil.

   (____,____)   (____,____)   (____,____)   (____,____)

9. Describe the change from the original quadrilateral to this new quadrilateral. Make a prediction. What would happen if you only changed the y-coordinates?

Chapter 4: The Contemporary Firsts

Dr. Christina Eubanks-Turner

"One of my ultimate goals as a mathematics educator is to diminish negative attitudes toward math in younger and older generations, especially in underrepresented groups. I will work tirelessly in teaching people that mathematics is a fundamental field of inquiry within the reach of anyone's comprehension".

Christina Eubanks-Turner is an associate professor of mathematics at Loyola Marymount University. She earned a bachelor of science degree in mathematics from Xavier University of Louisiana and both her master of science degree and Ph.D. in mathematics from the University of Nebraska-Lincoln, where she was one of the first two African Americans to receive doctorate degrees in mathematics from that institution.

She joined the Loyola Marymount University community in 2013, and in 2017 she achieved another first by being one of the first two African Americans to receive tenure and promotion in Loyola Marymount University's College of Science and Engineering. Her mathematical interests have not only theoretical and applicable implications, but also social implications. She primarily works in the areas of commutative algebra, mathematics education, and graph theory.

As a STEM educator, Dr. Eubanks-Turner works to broaden participation of underrepresented groups in the mathematical sciences. Some of her efforts include serving as principal investigator of government-funded projects on strengthening the STEM (Science, Technology, Engineering, and Mathematics) pipeline and holding membership on committees and boards that promote the achievement of women and people of color in STEM. One of her most important and rewarding endeavors in STEM is serving as a mentor and research advisor for both undergraduate and graduate students interested in mathematics. She mentors and works with young girls to let them know anyone can do math. As the mother of two phenomenal daughters, she encourages them daily to strive to do their best and not to let anyone limit their dreams and goals because of the color of their skin or their gender.

Pattern Block Design

Color the shapes so that you have a picture that shows symmetry. Name the shapes.

_____

_____

_____

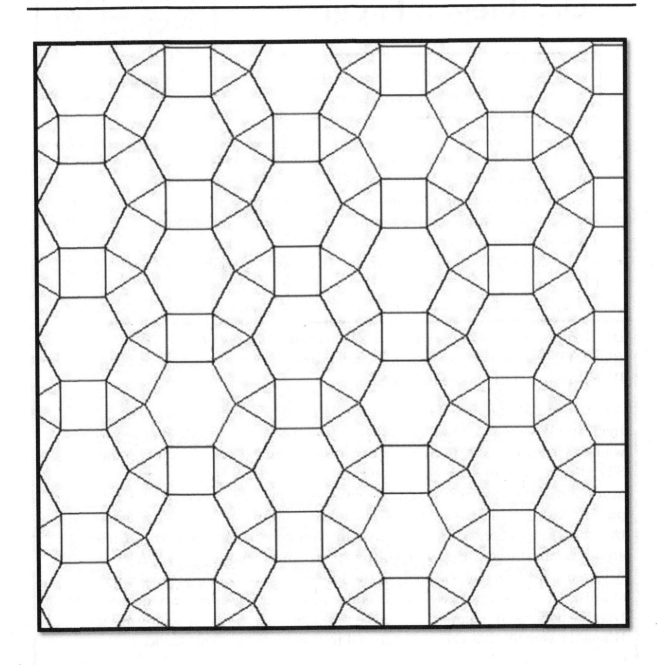

Dr. Raegan Higgins

"It is important we show children
who and what they can be".

- One of the first two African American women to earn doctoral degrees in mathematics from the University of Nebraska-Lincoln in 2008
- Associate professor of mathematics at Texas Tech University and the first African American to receive tenure and promotion in the mathematics and statistics department
- Co-director of the EDGE (Enhancing Diversity in Graduate Education) Program

Dr. Higgins is one of four creators of the website *Mathematically Gifted and Black*. The mission of the website is to feature and share the accomplishments of Blacks in the mathematical sciences.

A native of Baton Rouge, Louisiana, Dr. Higgins was named one of the 2016 Inspiring Women in STEM by *INSIGHT Into Diversity*. This award recognizes women who work to inspire and to encourage the next generation to pursue STEM education and careers via teaching, mentoring, research, and groundbreaking discoveries and innovations. Because of her own experience pursuing a STEM degree at a historically Black university, Raegan understands the importance of creating supportive environments where underrepresented students can thrive. Dr. Higgins also recently received an NSF LS-AMP Pre-Alliance award. One of the goals of the LS-AMP is to increase the quality and quantity of students successfully completing STEM baccalaureate degrees. Dr. Higgins believes it is important to show women, especially African American and Hispanic women, that they can succeed in the mathematical sciences.

Raegan and her handsome husband, Dr. Kamau Oginga Siwatu, are the proud parents of two lovely children, Jalia and Tendaji.

Integer Race

Directions: Start with a negative two (-2) and add or subtract the given integer. Write each answer along the way. What is your final answer? Write your answer in the finish spot. Can you make up your own race?

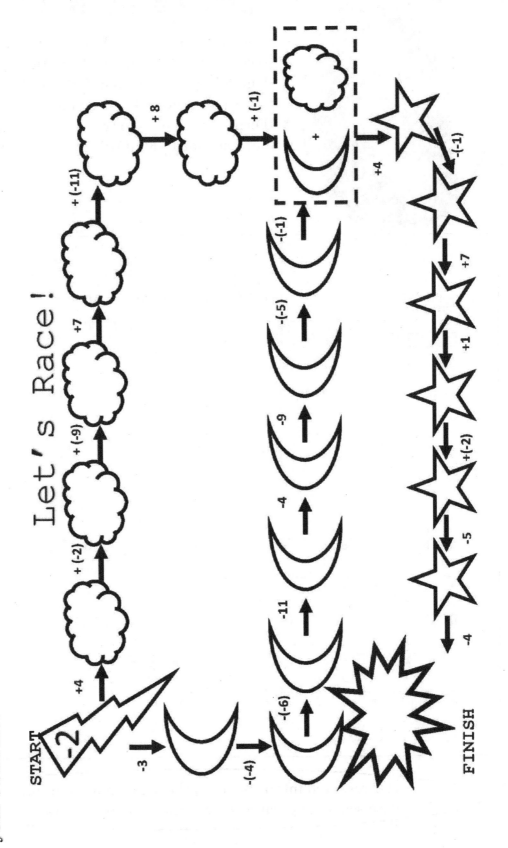

Let's Race!

START

FINISH

Dr. Tasha R. Inniss

★ One of the first three African American women to receive doctorates in mathematics from the University of Maryland, College Park
★ Associate provost for research at Spelman College
★ Formerly the director of education and industry outreach for INFORMS

Directions: Solve each math sentence to decode the message from Dr. Inniss. Match the result with a corresponding upper case letter and place in the corresponding place in the message. For example solve **b**; 5 + 6 = 11, the sum 11 corresponds to the upper case letter O. In the message put the letter O in all the blanks for **b**. The first one is done for you follow the pattern!

1	2	3	4	5	6	7	8	9	10	11	12	13	14	15	16	17	18	19	20	21
D	S	E	A	V	Y	R	F	M	K	O	N	I	W	P	U	G	T	L	C	H

a. 0 + 1 = __ ( )
b. 5 + 6 = __11__ (O)
c. 7 + 7 = __ ( )
d. 10 + 11 = __ ( )
e. 2 + 2 = __ ( )

f. 14 + 4 = __ ( )
g. 3 + 3 = __ ( )
h. 8 + 8 = __ ( )
i. 11 + 8 = __ ( )
j. 2 + 3 = __ ( )

k. 2 + 1 = __ ( )
l. 6 + 6 = __ ( )
m. 4 + 3 = __ ( )
n. 13 + 4 = __ ( )
o. 10 + 3 = __ ( )

p. 5 + 10 = __ ( )
q. 4 + 4 = __ ( )
r. 6 + 3 = __ ( )
s. 1 + 1 = __ ( )
t. 10 + 10 = __ ( )
u. 5 + 5 = __ ( )

__ _O_   __ __ __ __   __ _O_ __   __ _O_ __ __   __ __
a b   c d e f   g b h   i b j k   e l

__   __ __ __ __ __   __ __ __ __
a   l k j k m   n o j k

__ __   __ __ __ __   __ _O_ __   __ __ __   __ _O_
h p   c d k l   g b h   e m k   q b

__ __ _O_ __ __ __ __   __   __ __ __ __ __.
i i b c o l n   e   a m k e r

__ __ __ __ __ __ __ __ __ __   __ __   __ __
p k m s k j k m e l t k   o s   f d

__   __ __ __
k   u k g

Her research interests are in the areas of data mining, data science, operations research, and applied statistics.

Originally from New Orleans, Louisiana, Dr. Tasha Inniss graduated summa cum laude from Xavier University of Louisiana with a bachelor of science degree in mathematics. She earned a master of science degree in applied mathematics from the Georgia Institute of Technology and a Ph.D. in applied mathematics from the University of Maryland, College Park. She has also been a tenured associate professor of mathematics at Spelman College, a liberal arts college for women in Atlanta, Georgia.

Do what you love and NEVER GIVE UP when you are following a dream. Perseverance is the key!

Dr. Inniss has a passion for teaching mathematics and encouraging undergraduate students to pursue degrees in STEM disciplines. She was the principal investigator (PI) and director of a program at Spelman entitled "Mathematics Research and Mentoring Program", and led the development of and served as co-PI for Spelman's originally funded NSF HBCU-UP grant entitled "ASPIRE: Advancing Spelman's Participation in Informatics Research and Education".

Dr. Inniss has also served as the acting deputy division director of the Division of Human Resource Development in the Directorate of Education and Human Resources at the National Science Foundation.

When asked how she inspires young girls, she says she does it by taking advantage of as many opportunities as possible to talk to them about: how faith makes all things possible; how God gives them what they need to do what they love (and for her, that is math); how having supportive parents and encouraging teachers fills them with confidence and the strength to pursue their dreams; and how important it is never to give up!

Mathematics is the key to unlocking the mysteries and challenges in other scientific fields. The problem-solving part of mathematics is a lot of fun! Just think about all that you learn in mathematics as tools that you can use to help address some of the world's toughest problems. Using her particular areas of mathematics, namely operations research and analytics (which helps with quantitative decision-making), Dr. Inniss and her colleagues can create mathematical models for real-world situations and determine how to do things "better". In technical language, we refer to "better" as "optimal" or more efficient. We can also use data to figure out patterns to help us make decisions about the best next steps.

 Recipient of the Spelman College Presidential Award for Excellence in Teaching

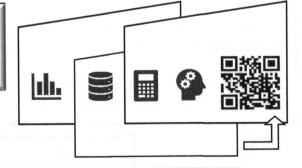

Learn how operations research, management sciences, and analytics relate to mathematics!

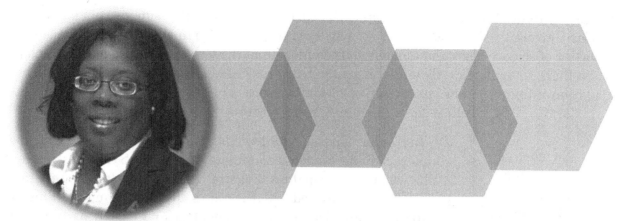

Dr. Monica Jackson

Dr. Monica Jackson was born and raised in Kansas City, Missouri. Mathematics was always her favorite subject in school. She loved doing math homework and learning about mathematics. Math has always been a big part of her life. Her earliest memory of loving math was at the age of six. She remembers doing math races with her family. She says, "My family would use a calculator and I would use pen and paper to solve simple problems. I loved getting the answer right and beating the calculator... or so I thought I was beating the calculator at the time ☺".

Monica received her bachelor of science degree in mathematics and master of science degree in applied mathematics from Clark Atlanta University in Atlanta, Georgia. She then received her Ph.D. in applied mathematics and scientific computation from the University of Maryland in 2003.

Dr. Jackson has been a teaching assistant, research assistant, and mathematics instructor at the University of Maryland, and completed post-doctoral research at Emory University in the department of biostatistics. She is an associate professor of statistics at American University in Washington, DC.

Her research interests are in the areas of spatial statistics and disease surveillance.

Dr. Jackson loves all kinds of dancing...salsa, ballet, jazz, etc. She is currently taking adult ballet lessons for fun.

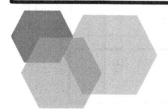

Can you make a prediction like a mathematician? How many smaller hexagons could fit inside the larger hexagon?

Spatial statistics is the study of things and the places where they are located.
Let us find out the states in which about half of the United States population lives.

Directions: Decode the words first to find out the states, and then match and color the location on the map!

0	1	2	3	4	5	6	7	8	9	10	11	12	13
G	W	E	C	O	D	H	K	R	X	Z	B	V	U

14	15	16	17	18	19	20	21	22	23	24	25		
P	M	N	T	J	L	S	I	A	Y	F	Q		

(1) 3 22 19 21 24 4 8 16 21 22

_____

(2) 17 2 9 22 20

_____

(3) 21 19 19 21 16 4 21 20

_____

(4) 15 21 3 6 21 0 22 16

_____

(5) 4 6 21 4

_____

(6) 14 2 16 16 20 23 19 12 22 16 21 22

_____

(7) 16 2 1   23 4 8 7

_____   _____

(8) 0 2 4 8 0 21 22

_____

(9) 24 19 4 8 21 5 22

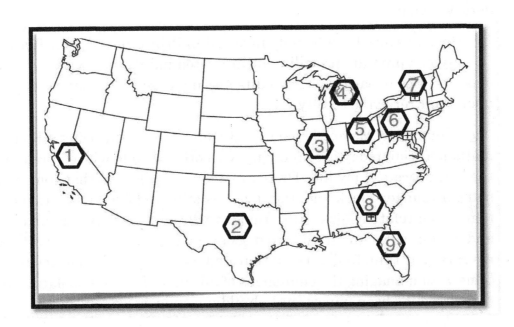

Dr. Talea Mayo

- Assistant professor,
  department of civil, environmental, and
  construction engineering,
  University of Central Florida
- Specializes in coastal ocean modeling,
  with special interests in hurricane storm
  surge modeling, risk analysis,
  and statistical data assimilation
  methods for state and parameter
  estimation

Though formally a mathematician, Dr. Mayo is very interested in applying mathematics to real-world problems. Specifically, she is interested in numerical modeling of coastal inundation due to tides and hurricane storm surges.

While in college, Dr. Mayo worked for NCAA Academic Enhancement as a mathematics tutor. It was then that she first learned the importance of building strong mathematical foundations.

She currently works to counteract this widespread issue by teaching extracurricular mathematics to high school girls in the central New Jersey region.

Dr. Mayo has also been heavily involved in Princeton's Prison Teaching Initiative, a program providing incarcerated individuals with opportunities to earn college credits and increase their chances of success upon their return to society.

According to Dr. Mayo, "The most difficult thing about being a Black mathematician today is connecting with other people who can relate to the many facets of my life. There are a lot of challenges that come with being a younger Black scientist. I can usually find friends to discuss family and relationships with, friends to discuss Black American culture and politics with, and friends to discuss my career and science with, but it's rare that I can find a friend that understands the difficulties that come with managing the challenges of all three. It can be isolating at times, and it's been important to build my support system".

Palindrome Magic!

A palindrome is a group of letters or numbers that reads the same forward and backward. For example, palindrome words are: wow, noon, radar, and racecar. Palindrome numbers are: 131, 6556, and 92329.

1. Create a list of palindrome words. What is the longest palindrome word you can think of (on your own!)?

   _____,_____

2. Create a list of palindrome numbers. What is the longest palindrome number you can think of (on your own!)?

   _____,_____

3. Just for fun, think of a list of palindrome dates. For example, July 10, 2017, is a palindrome date because it can be written forward and backward as 7102017.

4. What about palindrome years like 1881, 1991, and 2002? Name other palindrome years.

   _____,_____

5. Create palindrome numbers with addition. Choose a number. Turn it around and add to the original number. Is it a palindrome yet? If not, turn it around again and add. Most numbers will work, but it is not always easy! Some numbers must be reversed and added hundreds of times before making a palindrome. Try it!

   • For example: 47 + 74 = 121, which is a palindrome!

   • Let's try 69. How many steps does it take to get a palindrome?

     69 + 96 = 165; 165 + 561 = 726; 726 + 627 = 1353;

     1353 + 3531 = 4884, a palindrome! It took 4 steps!

Your turn! Keep trying until you find how many steps it takes to make your own palindrome.

Your number _____   How many steps? _____

Your palindrome _____

Dr. Yolanda Parker
Mathematics Teacher Educator

"The earlier our students are exposed to higher mathematics, the more prepared they will be for STEM fields".

Dr. Yolanda Parker's education includes earning a bachelor of science degree from Texas A&M University in applied mathematical sciences, a master of arts in liberal studies from Dartmouth College, and a Ph.D. in mathematics education from Illinois State University. Dr. Parker holds a Texas State Teaching Certificate in secondary mathematics and taught middle school mathematics and computer literacy prior to earning her graduate degrees.

Dr. Parker is currently a professor in the mathematics department at Tarrant County College-South Campus where she primarily teaches statistics, college algebra, developmental mathematics, and mathematics content courses for teachers. She recently received the Chancellor's Award for Exemplary Teaching at Tarrant County College. Dr. Parker enjoys conducting professional development workshops and presenting at professional conferences. She enjoys learning about effective teaching methods and strategies in mathematics classrooms and sharing those ideas with practicing teachers. She is interested in researching culturally relevant teaching in mathematics. Dr. Parker likes having fun in her mathematics class and says she is known for posting something about Pi Day and Pi Approximation Day each year on social media. She engages her students in some activity each year that involves circles and ends with a round treat (usually oatmeal pies).

Dr. Parker was honored by the Dallas-Fort Worth Professionals Chapter of NSBE (National Society of Black Engineers) in the inaugural class of ten "Hidden Figures of Dallas: Top Women of Color in STEM" in 2017.

She is happily married to Claud Parker–her best friend and favorite jazz saxophonist– and is mother to one son, Claud, Jr.

$3.14159 26$

Lemon Pi(e)

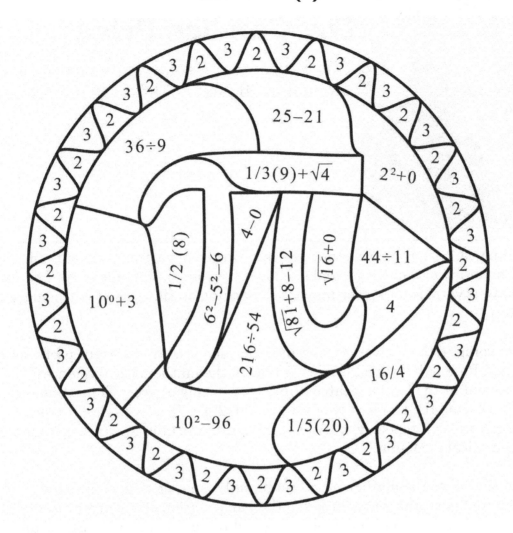

1. Simplify the expressions in the circle.
2. Color the circle using the following colors:
   a. 2's are Light Brown
   b. 3's are Dark Brown
   c. 4's are Yellow
   d. 5's are Red
3. Name the special symbol in the circle. _____
4. What is the meaning of the symbol? _____
5. Do you like pie? _____ What is your favorite pie? _____

$5\ 3\ ^5\ _8\ 9\ 7\ ^9\ 3\ ^2\ 3...$

Dr. Candice Price

"Diversity of representative images of Black women in all facets of life is so important for all".

Dr. Candice Price is an assistant professor in the department of mathematics at the University of San Diego, and she loves how one problem in mathematics can have several solutions or impacts depending on the area of mathematics involved.

Before going to the University of San Diego, she was an assistant professor and National Research Council Davies Fellow in the mathematical sciences department at the United States Military Academy at West Point. She received her Ph.D. from the University of Iowa in 2012. Dr. Price's research area is primarily in DNA topology, but she is currently working in various areas of mathematical modeling.

In her service to the mathematical community, she seeks to create and contribute to programs that broaden the participation of underrepresented groups by focusing on strong mentoring and research networks. She is an architect behind the *Mathematically Gifted and Black* website and is on the organizing committee for Underrepresented Students in Topology and Algebra Research Symposium (USTARS).

Dr. Price says, "One of my proudest accomplishments has been staying active in issues of underrepresentation in mathematics by creating and participating in programs that focus on enhancing the participation of underrepresented groups. It is no easy feat to stay active in service while also moving forward in the directions of better teaching and innovative research; and, while I am not yet where I want to be, I am constantly learning, improving, and moving forward".

Solve the Shapes Puzzle

Write the correct numbers in the shapes to solve the number sentences.

1.   5   x   ☐   = 20

2.   ☐   x   ◯   = 320

3.   ◯   x   △   = 160

4.   △   x   ☐   =   ⬡

5.   120   ÷   ⬠   = 12

☐ = _____,   ◯ = _____,

△ = _____,   ⬡ = _____,   ⬠ = _____

Mathematics and More Crossword Puzzle

Conduct your own research to answer the questions below and then complete the crossword puzzle.

Across

1. Prior to 1958, the National Aeronautics and Space Administration (NASA) was called?

3. The first African American woman to earn a doctorate in mathematics from Yale University in New Haven, CT

6. A prize awarded to young mathematicians presented by the International Mathematical Union (IMU)

7. A group of letters or numbers that reads the same forward and backward

8. A pattern that repeats with no gaps or overlaps

16. This mathematician established a computer science program at Spelman College in Atlanta, GA

17. This actress played Mary Jackson in the movie *Hidden Figures*

18. A six-sided polygon

19. The first African American woman to earn a doctorate in mathematics

Down

2. Argelia Velez-Rodriguez's country of birth

4. A transformation that places the object directly on top of itself

5. The first woman of color to go into space on the shuttle Endeavor in 1992

7. The ratio of the circumference and diameter of a circle

9. The author of the groundbreaking book *Hidden Figures*

10. The study of the relationship between mathematics and culture

11. A triangle with exactly two congruent sides

12. In 1943, Dorothy Vaughan was hired at this research center in Virginia

13. Women's History Month

14. Which Hidden Figure devoted much of her NASA career to researching supersonic flight and sonic boom?

15. A segregated high school turned museum in Farmville, Virginia

Mathematics and More Crossword Puzzle

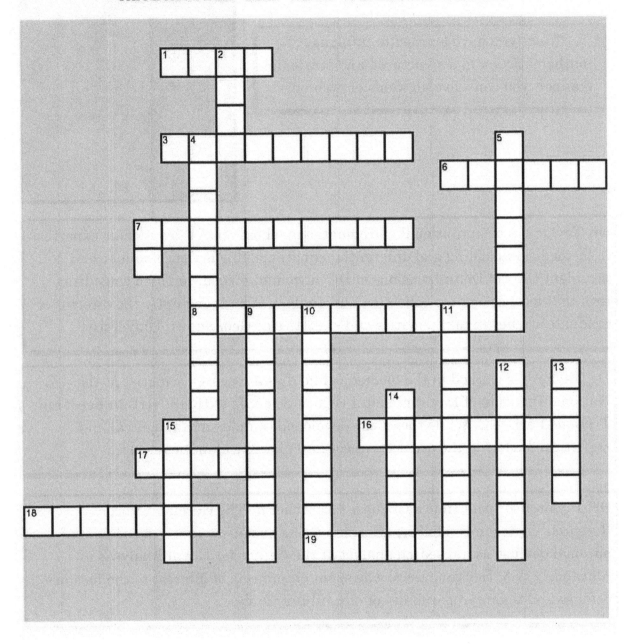

Dr. Shree W. Taylor

"Once you have learned to think as a mathematician, in a structured and strategic manner, you can solve all kinds of problems".

Dr. Taylor is a computational mathematician whose specialties include expertise in biomedical modeling and differential equations. She is the cofounder and president/CEO of Delta Decisions of DC, a woman-owned, certified consulting firm that focuses on data collection and analysis. She is currently the director of graduate studies in mathematics and statistics at Georgetown University.

Dr. Taylor has worked in the biomedical field as a research scientist at the National Institute of Environmental Health Sciences (NIEHS/NIH) in Research Triangle Park, NC. While there, she developed complex mathematical and statistical models in the areas of cancer and pharmacokinetic research.

Dr. Taylor also spent time as a guest researcher at The German Cancer Research Center in Heidelberg, Germany. She has also worked in the field of national defense as a research analyst at the Center for Naval Analyses in Alexandria, VA. Her time there was spent on projects of interest to the nation's defense and the interoperability of our military forces.

* Ph.D. in applied mathematics, North Carolina State University
* Bachelor of science and master of science in mathematics, Clark Atlanta University

Directions: The words below are among the many that describe Dr. Shree W. Taylor, as well as some of her interests. Find the words in the word search.

Have fun!

research   children   education   environment   health   science
dr taylor   data   solution   help   loyal   spanish
german   mathematics   volunteer   analyst

e	d	u	c	a	t	i	o	n	b	f	j
g	n	a	l	k	w	z	x	p	q	q	m
n	y	v	o	l	u	n	t	e	e	r	a
d	c	h	i	l	d	r	e	n	l	p	t
s	k	u	v	r	e	s	e	a	r	c	h
a	p	t	s	l	o	y	a	l	v	d	e
g	p	a	o	v	x	n	z	g	o	n	m
e	f	b	n	l	c	f	m	a	z	i	a
r	o	c	a	i	k	s	h	e	l	p	t
m	t	t	z	y	s	l	w	q	n	a	i
a	h	t	l	a	e	h	c	a	v	t	c
n	v	o	a	n	o	i	t	u	l	o	s
k	l	t	p	a	n	a	l	y	s	t	d
q	a	m	n	s	c	i	e	n	c	e	c
d	r	t	a	y	l	o	r	u	i	o	v

Dr. Erica N. Walker

Professor of mathematics education
Teachers College,
Columbia University

"I am a former high school mathematics teacher who has always loved teaching and talking about mathematics. The people who have most influenced me have been teachers: from my very first teachers, my parents; to my childhood neighbors (many of whom were career schoolteachers and professors); to elementary, secondary, college, and graduate school teachers and professors. All of these people instilled in me a love of learning and underscored daily that learning is something to be enjoyed, and it is something you never stop doing. I hope to share this love of learning with everyone with whom I am privileged to work".

Dr. Walker earned a bachelor's degree in mathematics with a minor in Spanish from Birmingham-Southern College in Birmingham, Alabama, and a master's degree in mathematics education from Wake Forest University in Winston-Salem, North Carolina. She earned her doctorate in education from Harvard University in Cambridge, Massachusetts.

She collaborates with teachers, schools, districts, and organizations to promote mathematics excellence and equity for young people. Dr. Walker is also the author of two books and the recipient of two prestigious awards including the Association for Women in Mathematics and the Mathematical Association of America Etta Zuber Falconer Lecture in 2015 and the National Association of Mathematicians Award of Appreciation for her 2018 Cox-Talbot Lecture.

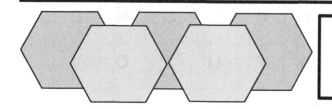

The beauty of math can be seen in nature. Color the beautiful flower on the next page to show its symmetry.

Dr. Chelsea Walton

Chelsea Walton was born and raised in Detroit, Michigan, and attended Detroit Public Schools. She learned that she could make a career out of her lifelong interest in and aptitude for mathematics when her senior year calculus instructor introduced her to the possibility of becoming a mathematician.

Dr. Walton attended Michigan State University (MSU) and graduated in 2005 with a bachelor's degree in mathematics. After her second year of graduate school at MSU, Chelsea was given the opportunity to complete her research work at the University of Manchester in England.

After earning a Ph.D. in mathematics from the University of Michigan, Dr. Walton completed a National Science Foundation postdoc at the University of Washington in Seattle and then became the Moore Instructor in the mathematics department at MIT.

Outreach is very important to Dr. Walton. She taught for the EDGE Program, which aims to strengthen the ability of women students to successfully complete Ph.D. programs in the mathematical sciences. She was named as a 2017 Sloan Research Fellow. This is a highly competitive and prestigious honor.

Dr. Chelsea Walton lives with her husband and two dogs, Mr. Mischief Maker (a gray Boston terrier) and Dr. Boom Boom (a black pug), in Urbana, Illinois. She enjoys streaming TV and movies, and she often uses TV as background noise for work. *Lost* and *Lord of the Rings* are some of her go-tos for this type of background noise.

Function Fun

Are you ready for algebra? Find the words and say yes!

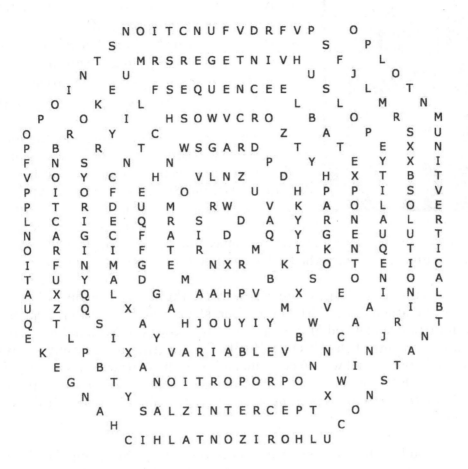

```
              N O I T C N U F V D R F V P       O
          S                                 S       P
       T       M R S R E G E T N I V H     F     L
     N       U                         U     J     O
       I     E       F S E Q U E N C E E     S     L       T
   O       K       L                 L     L     M     N
 P       O       I       H S O W V C R O     B     O     R     M
O     R       Y       C             Z     A     P     S     U
O   B       R     T       W S G A R D     T     T     E   X X   N
F   N   S     N     N           P     Y     E   Y   X   I
V   O   Y   C     H     V L N Z     D     H   X   T   B   T
P   I   O   F   E     O       U     H   P   P   I   S   V
P   T   R   D   U   M     R W   V   K   A   O   L   O   E
L   C   I   E   Q   R   S   D   A   Y   R   N   A   L   R
N   A   G   C   F   A   I   D   Q   Y   G   E   U   U   T
O   R   I   I   F   T   R   M   I   K   E   N   Q   T   I
I   F   N   M   G   E   N X R   K   O   T   O   E   I   C
T   U   Y   A   D   M       B   S   N   O   N   N   O   A
A   X   Q   L   G     A A H P V   X   E   I   N   I   L
U   Z   Q     X     A         M     V     A     R     B
Q   T   S       A     H J O U Y I Y     W     A     R     T
E     L     I     Y               B     C     J     N
  K       P     X     V A R I A B L E V   N   N     A
    E     B     A                 N   I   T
      G     T     N O I T R O P O R P O     W     S
        N     Y                       X     N
          A     S A L Z I N T E R C E P T     O
            H                             C
              C I H L A T N O Z I R O H L U
```

WORD LIST:

AXIS	FUNCTION	PLOT	TABLE
CHANGE	GRAPH	POINTS	UNIT
CONSTANT	HORIZONTAL	PROPORTION	VARIABLE
DECIMAL	INEQUALITY	RATE	VERTICAL
EQUATION	INTEGERS	SEQUENCE	
EXPONENT	INTERCEPT	SLOPE	
FRACTION	ORIGIN	SOLUTION	

Dr. Talitha M. Washington

- Associate professor of mathematics, Howard University, Washington, DC
- Program officer, National Science Foundation (NSF), Division of Undergraduate Education
- Ph.D. in mathematics, specialization in applied mathematics, University of Connecticut (UCONN)

Dr. Washington grew up in Evansville, Indiana, and graduated from Bosse High School a semester early and studied abroad in Costa Rica for six months on an exchange program. She graduated from Spelman College with a degree in mathematics before attending the University of Connecticut as a graduate student. Dr. Washington faced many obstacles along the way, but she met them with resilience and determination. Diligently, she worked night and day to learn the background material necessary for success.

While in graduate school, Talitha enjoyed working through mathematical problems and applications of mathematics. With her advisor, she researched a theoretical protein-protein interaction model and also became involved with the National Resource for Cell Analysis and Modeling at the UCONN Health Center. After graduating, she researched a hormone secretion model with faculty members in the mathematics and cell biology departments at Duke University. With her applied background, she led various undergraduate research projects from modeling the Tacoma Narrows Bridge to modeling calcium homeostasis.

With her passion for education, she led a youth conference, *Stepping Up*, which encouraged youths to pursue viable careers through higher education. She also led a one-week research-based summer camp for middle schoolers to explore current trends in mathematics and the sciences. In her spare time, she serves on many boards and regularly seeks remedies for various inequity issues in education. Among many awards, Dr. Washington received the 2019 Black Engineer of the Year (BEYA) STEM Innovator Award. She balances stress by maintaining a rigorous exercise regimen that includes step aerobics, kickboxing, strength training, and yoga. Dr. Washington is mom to three vivacious STEM teenagers.

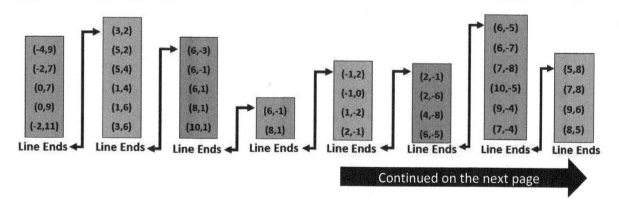

Continued on the next page

Blast Off! Plot the points and name the picture.

Line Ends	Line Ends		Line Ends		Name of Picture is?
(8,5)	(11,0)	(6,-5)	(-10,20)	(-14,21)	(-11,12)
(13,5)	(13,0)	(12,1)	(-12,20)	(-14,20)	(-7,8)
(15,3)	(14,-1)	(8,5)	(-13,21)	(-13,19)	(-1,2)
(12,1)	(11,-4)	(5,8)	(-14,21)	(-13,17)	(2,-1)
	(10,-3)	0,13)	(-16,23)	(-11,15)	(6,-5)
	(10,-1)	(-5,18)			
		(-8,18)			

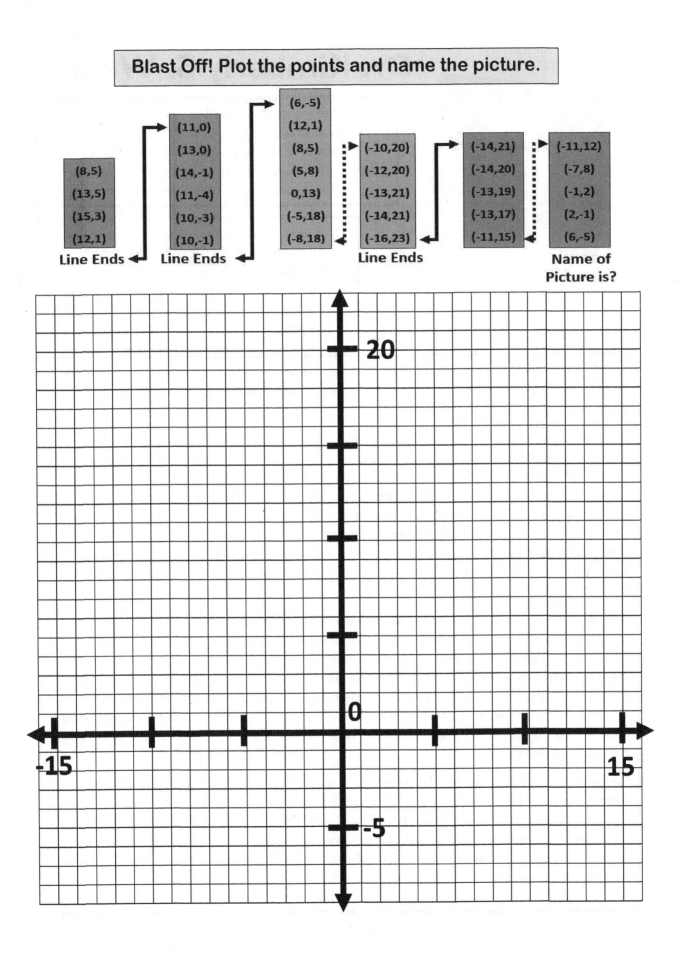

20

0

-15   15

-5

97

Dr. Kimberly S. Weems

"One of my most rewarding experiences is co-organizing the first Infinite Possibilities Conference (IPC), which was started by two Spelman College alumnae and mathematicians, Drs. Leona Harris and Tanya Moore".

- Kimberly S. Weems is associate professor of mathematics at North Carolina Central University (NCCU).
- Dr. Weems is the 2017 recipient of the College of Arts and Sciences Excellence in Teaching Award.

Dr. Weems's research interests include statistical models for count data. Since joining NCCU in 2015, she has been instrumental in enhancing its graduate mathematics curriculum with statistics courses.

Weems is a native of Cartersville, Georgia. As a teenager, she competed in mathematics quiz bowls and participated in summer mathematics enrichment programs. After graduating from high school, Weems entered Spelman College in Atlanta, Georgia, where she earned a bachelor of science degree in mathematics with a minor in Spanish. Afterwards, she earned her master of arts degree and a Ph.D. in mathematics from the University of Maryland, College Park. She completed postdoctoral studies in the statistics department at North Carolina State University, where she later joined the faculty and served for two years as co-director of statistics graduate programs until moving to NCCU.

As a mother of two daughters, Dr. Weems strives to inspire them to enjoy and appreciate mathematics every day. Whenever possible, she takes them with her to meetings and workshops, especially those that celebrate diversity in mathematics. She uses the influence of her own mother, Kansadie Stewart Weems, who inspired her love for mathematics. Her mother taught mostly biology and some mathematics in the Georgia public school system. As a child, Kimberly spent countless afternoons "playing school" with her mother's mathematics textbooks, and she traveled with her mother to regional science fairs.

Dr. Weems is most known for being one of three—along with Drs. Tasha Inniss and Sherry Scott—who became the first African American women to earn doctorate degrees in mathematics from the University of Maryland, College Park. She is a member of the American Statistical Association and the National Association of Mathematicians as well as an advisory board member of the Infinite Possibilities Conference for women of color in mathematics.

Statistics Words to Know

Please unscramble the words below.

Scrambled Word	Unscrambled Word – Statistics Vocabulary
1. AGHPR	
2. MANE	
3. MADINE	
4. MDEO	
5. GNRAE	
6. EOTIULR	
7. MUIINMM	
8. MUXAIMM	
9. LEAIUQRT	
10. QAAITEVULIT	
11. NVIEUIATTTAQ	
12. RNDOAM	
13. SBAI	
14. ATDA	
15. AMPLES	
16. PPOAOITNLU	

Dr. Shelby Wilson

Originally from Milledgeville, Georgia, Shelby grew up loving mathematics and puzzles of all kinds. After graduating from high school, she entered Spelman College. It was at Spelman that Shelby learned that she could turn her love of math into a profession.

Shelby received a B.S. in mathematics and computer science from Spelman College in 2006 and then moved on to graduate school within the applied mathematics (AMSC) program at the University of Maryland, College Park. She did her graduate research in the field of mathematical biology under the direction of Professor Doron Levy. She earned two degrees in applied mathematics from the University of Maryland: a master's degree in 2010 and a doctorate degree in 2012. After finishing her Ph.D. she continued her research as a postdoctoral fellow at INRIA (Institut National de Recherche en Informatique et en Automatique) in Grenoble, France. This gave Shelby the opportunity to further explore a number of her passions: mathematics, good food, and traveling.

In January 2014, Dr. Wilson became an assistant professor in the mathematics department of Morehouse College in Atlanta, Georgia. There, she works toward preparing the next generation of great thinkers.

Dr. Wilson's research focuses on exploring mathematical problems with applications in the medical sciences (e.g., how much and when should we administer certain medicines?).

In her spare time, Shelby enjoys reading, traveling abroad, playing basketball, and eating at great restaurants.

I SPY

Find the following unlikely items to be found in a science lab. Circle the items:
Basketball, birthday cake, candy/lollipop, jelly jar, key, peace sign, pizza, smiley
face, snail, snake, spaghetti & meatballs, superhero book, and worm. Color the
picture.

Selected Activity Answer Keys

African American Women Mathematicians Word Search Key

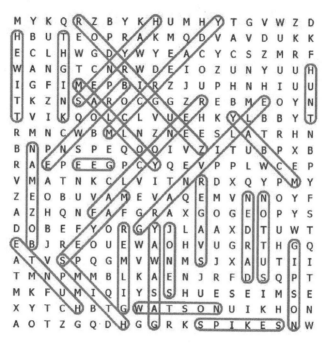

M Y K Q R Z B Y K H U M H Y T G V W Z D
H B U T E O P R A K M O D V A V D U K K
E C L H W G D Y W Y E A C Y C S Z M R F
W A N G T C N R W D E I O Z U N Y U U H
I G F I M E P B I R Z J U P H N H I U U
T K Z N S A R O C G G Z R E B M E O Y N
T V I K Q O L C L V U E H K Y L B B Y T
R M N C W B M L N Z N E E S L A T R H N
B N P N S P E Q O O I V Z I T U B P X B
R A E P E E G P C Y Q E V P P L W C E P
V M A T N K C L V I T N R D X Q Y P M Y
Z E O B U V A M E V A Q E M N N O Y F
A Z H Q N F A F G R A X G O G E O P Y S
D O B E F Y O R G Y J L A A X D T U W T
E B J R E O U E W A O H V U G R T H G Q
A T V S P Q G M V W N M S J X A U T I I
T M N P M M B L K A E N J R F D S Q P T
M K F U M I Q I Y S S H U E S E I M S E
X Y T C H B T G W A T S O N U I K H O N
A O T Z G Q D H G G R K S P I K E S N W

WORD LIST:

BOZEMAN	GIPSON	KNIGHT	SPIKES
BROWNE	GRANVILLE	MALLOY	SUTTON
DARDEN	HAYNES	MAYES	SVAGER
FALCONER	HEWITT	MCBAY	WATSON
GASAWAY	HUNT	MCCREADY	
GEE	HUNTE	RODRIGUEZ	
GILMER	JONES	SMITH	

Connect the Coordinate Points – Key

Using the map below and the coordinate plane, complete the following tasks:

Task 1
Using a dark pencil, plot the following points and connect them in the order that they are plotted. This will provide you with the outline of Washington, DC.

(-6.5, 3.8); (-1.2, 9); (7.2, 0); (-1, -9); (-1, -5);
(-0.8, -4); (-1.5, -2); (-6.5, 3.8)

Task 2
Use a different colored pencil for each location below. Plot and label the points representing the schools that Dr. Haynes attended or taught at in Washington, DC.

A. Armstrong High School: Point A (0.5, 1.5)
B. Catholic University of America: Point B (1.5, 4.5)
C. M Street High School: Point C (0.5, 2)
D. Miner Normal School: Point D (-0.3, 2.5)
E. Miner Teachers College (University of District of Columbia): Point E (-3.5, 4.5)
F. Smith College: Point F (-1.5, 2.5)

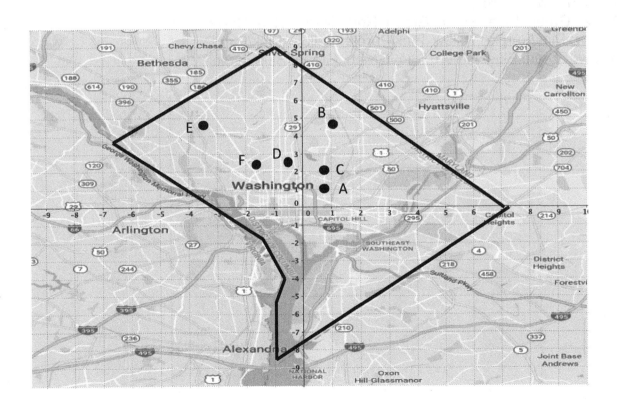

NASA Facts – Key

What is the name of the oldest artificial satellite still in space today?

<u>V</u> <u>A</u> <u>N</u> <u>G</u> <u>U</u> <u>A</u> <u>R</u> <u>D</u> <u>1</u>

1   23   19   5   11   13   12   4   7

Which NASA program launched the first Americans into space?

<u>P</u> <u>R</u> <u>O</u> <u>J</u> <u>E</u> <u>C</u> <u>T</u> <u>M</u> <u>E</u> <u>R</u> <u>C</u> <u>U</u> <u>R</u> <u>Y</u>

9   2   15   17   18   20   16   10   8   22   14   21   3   6

Color by Shape! – Key

Colors in order by row:
1st row: Green, Blue, Green, Green, Red, Green, Blue, Green
2nd row: Pink/Purple, Yellow, Pink/Purple, Yellow, Pink/Purple
3rd row: Green, Blue, Green, Red, Green, Green, Blue, Green

Geometry Word Search - Key

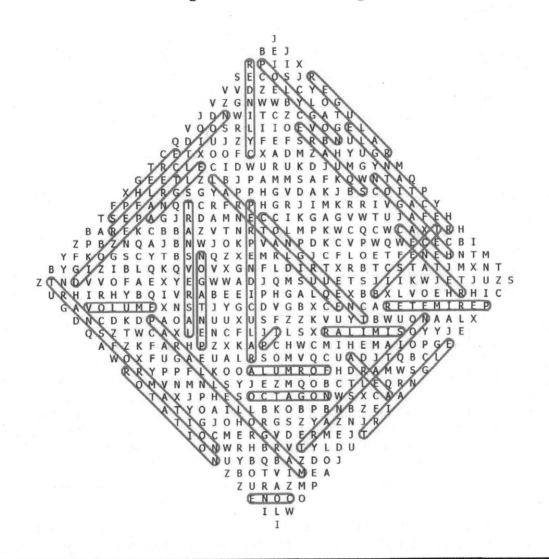

Fun with Magic Squares – Key

There are different types of magic squares, and they are very fun to think about. For example, the square below becomes a magic square if you can use the numbers 1–9, only once each, to fill the square so that every row, column, and diagonal has a sum of 15. Try it!

8	3	4
1	5	9
6	7	2

4	9	2
3	5	7
8	1	6

1. Sample responses: Opposite corners have a sum of 10. The nine numbers have a sum of 45.

2. Yes, there are eight 3x3 magic squares that have columns and rows with sums of 15.

3. A possible strategy is to add the consecutive numbers from 10 to 18 and then divide the sum, 126, by 3.

15	10	17
16	14	12
11	18	13

There are strategies to creating magic squares. If this is something that interests you, look it up and learn some useful strategies. For example, if you create an 8x8 magic square, you will need 64 boxes, therefore 64 numbers. If you use the numbers 1 to 64, so that each row, column, and diagonal adds up to the same number, it turns out that the number is the sum of the 64 consecutive numbers you use. In this case, 1 + 2 + 3 + ... + 63 + 64 = 260. Therefore, the magic number for an 8x8 magic square that goes from 1 to 64 is 260. Try it!

4. Another type of magic square is one where every row, column, and diagonal has the same product! For example, the magic square below has a magic product of 1000. Complete the magic square using the nine divisors of 100.

5	4	50
100	10	1
2	25	20

5. Answers will vary.

Euler Graphs: Paths and Circuits – Key

III. A graph is called an Euler graph if it has an Euler circuit. Tell whether each of these graphs has an Euler path, an Euler circuit, or neither. Write the path for each.

a.

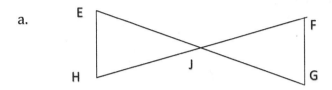

One circuit is EJGFJHE. Are there more?

b.

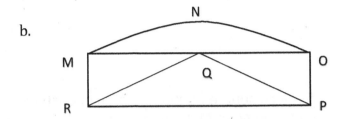

Neither a path nor a circuit can be found. Can you think of a reason why?

c.

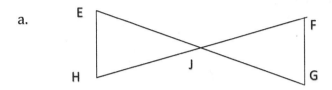

One path is UWYXWSTUS. Are there more?

IV. Create/draw an Euler path that is not a circuit. Draw an Euler circuit. Answers will vary.

Magic Squares Challenge – Key

1. There are different types of magic squares, and they are very fun to think about. For example, the 4x4 square below becomes a magic square if you can complete it using the numbers from 1–16 only once so every row, column, and diagonal has the same sum. What is the magic sum?

16	2	3	13
5	11	10	8
9	7	6	12
4	14	15	1

2. Write the numbers 1 to 25 in the 5x5 magic square so that the sum of each row, column, and diagonal is 65. Look up the Siamese Method for help.

17	24	1	8	15
23	5	7	14	16
4	6	13	20	22
10	12	19	21	3
11	18	25	2	9

3. Answers will vary.

Quadrilateral Transformations – Key

1. Number the x- and y-axes. Plot the ordered pairs on the grid below and then connect the points to create a quadrilateral. (4, 13); (11, 8); (7, 13); (4, 8)
2. Name the quadrilateral. <u>Trapezoid</u>
3. Double the x- and y-coordinates and plot the new points on the same grid below.
   (8, 26)   (22, 16)   (14, 26)   (8, 16)
4. What happened to the size of the quadrilateral after you doubled the coordinates?
   <u>The size of the quadrilateral quadrupled.</u>
5. What is the area of the original quadrilateral? <u>25 square units</u>
6. What is the area of the enlarged quadrilateral? <u>100 square units</u>
7. What does this tell you? <u>The area quadrupled.</u>
8. Double the x-coordinates only. Keep the y-coordinates the same. Plot the new points. Hint: Use a different color pen or pencil.
   (8, 13)   (22, 8)   (14, 13)   (8, 8)
9. Describe the change from the original quadrilateral to this new quadrilateral. Make a prediction. What would happen if you only changed the y-coordinates?
   <u>The size (or area) doubled. The new shape is 2 times wider.</u>
   <u>The shape with the doubled y-coordinates would be 2 times taller and the area would be</u>
   <u>doubled.</u>

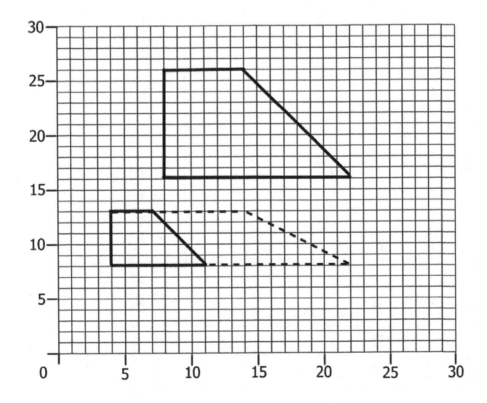

111

Decode the Message about Dorothy Vaughan – Key

	27÷9	6x6	54÷9	14÷2	18÷6		24÷3	2x5	24÷2	20÷5	5x6	2x4	24÷6	35÷5
Row 1	= 3	= 36	= 6	= 7	= 3		= 8	= 10	= 12	= 4	= 30	= 8	= 4	= 7
Row 2	3x8	36÷12	6x6	7x6	3x5		8x9	10x6	12x3	4x4	30÷10	8x7	4x8	7x3
	=	=	=	=	=		=	=	=	=	=	=	=	=
Row 3	24	3	36	42	15		72	60	36	16	3	56	32	21
Row 4	H	U	M	A	N		C	O	M	P	U	T	E	R

What did you find out about Dorothy Vaughan?
Dorothy Vaughan was a HUMAN COMPUTER.

What's That Word? – Key

Equation	Solution	Solution's corresponding letter
$40 \div (3 + 5)$	5	E
$\dfrac{60}{3}$	20	T
$2 + 2 \times 3$	8	H
$2 \times (3 + 4)$	14	N
$\left(\dfrac{15}{3}\right) \times 3$	15	O
$1 + 1 + 2 \times 5 + 1$	13	M
12^0	1	A
$2 \times 2 \times 10 \div 2$	20	T
2^3	8	H
$23^0 \times 10 \div 2$	5	E
$\dfrac{69}{3} - 10$	13	M
$7 \times 8 \div 56$	1	A
$2 \times 2 \times 5$	20	T
$(18 \div 6)^2$	9	I
$\dfrac{27}{3^2}$	3	C
$140 \div 7 - (8 - 7)$	19	S

Secret word and definition: **<u>Ethnomathematics</u>** <u>is the study of such mathematical ideas involved in the cultural practices of a people.</u>

Lucky You! Probability Word Search - Key

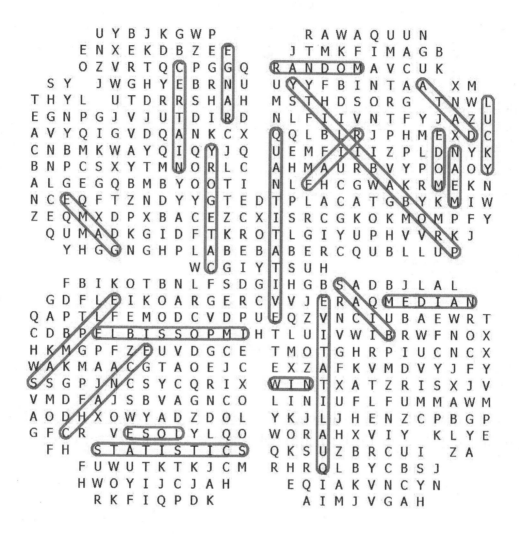

WORD LIST:

BIAS	GAME	MODE	SAMPLE
CATEGORY	IMPOSSIBLE	PROBABILITY	STATISTICS
CERTAIN	LOSE	QUALITATIVE	WIN
CHANCE	LUCKY	QUANTITATIVE	
DATA	MEAN	RANDOM	
FAIR	MEDIAN	RANGE	

Decode the Puzzle – Key

Dr. Genevieve Knight was a founding member of this organization founded in 1986. This organization is an advocate for African American children with respect to the learning and teaching of mathematics.

Alphabet Chart

A	B	C	D	E	F	G	H	I	J	K	L	M
1	2	3	4	5	6	7	8	9	10	11	12	13

N	O	P	Q	R	S	T	U	V	W	X	Y	Z
14	15	16	17	18	19	20	21	22	23	24	25	26

Number Expression	Result	Letter from Alphabet Chart	Actual (Decoded) Letter
$5^2 \div 0.5 - 30 + 4$	24	X	B
$1/3 \times 45 - 6$	9	I	M
$(1200 - 7 \times 10^{10})/50$	10	J	N
100^0	1	A	E
0.08×75	6	F	J
$(60 + 15) - (60 + 1)$	14	N	R
$3^3 - 4$	23	W	A
$7\frac{1}{2} \div 1\frac{1}{2}$	5	E	I
$\sqrt{49}$	7	G	K

Original Coded Message:

X	A	J	F	W	I	E	J		X	W	J	J	A	G	A	N
24	1	10	6	23	9	5	10		24	23	10	10	1	7	1	14

Decoded Message—Name of Organization:

B E N J A M I N   B A N N E K E R

Explain how you decoded the puzzle. Answers will vary.

Make up your own puzzle and play with a friend or family member.

Find the Treasure Chest – Key

Each answer below is a clue to which path to take.

a. $30 - 14 = \underline{16}$

b. $21 \div 3 = \underline{7}$

c. $5 \times 6 = \underline{30}$

d. $0 \times 99 = \underline{0}$

e. $(6 \times 6) + (6 + 7) = \underline{49}$

f. $10^2 - 1 = \underline{99}$

g. $46\frac{3}{4} + 1\frac{1}{4} = \underline{48}$

Benjamin Banneker Gears – Key

1. How many teeth does gear C have? $\underline{36}$
   How many teeth does gear D have? $\underline{6}$
2. If gear C makes two full rotations, how many full rotations does gear B make? $\underline{4}$
   How many full rotations does gear D make? $\underline{12}$

Mystery Shape Equations – Key

$\square$ = $\underline{5}$ $\bigcirc$ = $\underline{12}$ $\trapezoid$ = $\underline{3}$

Fraction Facts: Color the Planets – Key

Perform the operations below. Match the numerator answer with the planet in the table and denominator answer with the color code. Then color the planets above. Do not simplify.

Ex: $\frac{1}{2} + \frac{2}{2} = \frac{3}{2}$ The numerator is 3, which matches with Earth. The denominator is 2, which matches with light blue, so you would color the Earth light blue.

$\frac{1}{4} + \frac{5}{4} = \frac{6}{4}$ $\frac{3}{7} + \frac{2}{7} = \frac{5}{7}$ $\frac{1}{3} + \frac{1}{3} = \frac{2}{3}$

$\frac{8}{9} - \frac{1}{9} = \frac{7}{9}$ $\frac{9}{10} - \frac{5}{10} = \frac{4}{10}$ $\frac{12}{13} - \frac{11}{13} = \frac{1}{13}$

$\frac{5}{7} \times \frac{3}{2} = \frac{15}{14}$ $\frac{10}{11} \times \frac{5}{3} = \frac{50}{33}$ $\frac{1}{3} \times \frac{20}{13} = \frac{20}{39}$

Use the color codes as directed.

116

Sudoku Puzzle Fun – Key

2	8	5	6	9	7	1	4	3
1	3	4	8	2	5	6	7	9
9	7	6	1	3	4	5	2	8
5	2	7	3	6	9	4	8	1
6	1	3	2	4	8	7	9	5
4	9	8	7	5	1	3	6	2
8	4	9	5	1	6	2	3	7
7	5	2	4	8	3	9	1	6
3	6	1	9	7	2	8	5	4

Dr. Christine Darden Crossword - Key

Brain Buster – Key

Sonia	Teddy	Owen	Paola	Isabelle
First	Second	Third	Fourth	Fifth

Answer: Owen is in third place

Wind Tunnel Math – Key

Paths Starting with 2	Paths Starting with 3	Paths Starting with 4	Paths Starting with 5
2 * 3 * 1 − 4 − 5 = -3	3 + 5 − 4 ÷ 2 + 1 = 3	4 − 5 ÷ 1 + 2 * 3 = 3	5 − 4 − 1 + 2 * 3 = 6
2 * 3 + 5 − 4 − 1 = 6	3 + 5 ÷ 1 + 2 ÷ 4 = 2.5	4 − 5 + 3 * 2 + 1 = 5	5 − 4 ÷ 2 * 3 * 1 = 1.5
2 * 3 + 5 ÷ 1 − 4 = 7	3 + 5 ÷ 1 − 4 ÷ 2 = 2	4 − 5 + 3 * 1 + 2 = 4	5 − 4 ÷ 2 + 1 * 3 = 4.5
2 ÷ 4 − 5 + 3 * 1 = 0	3 + 5 − 4 − 1 + 2 = 5	4 ÷ 2 * 3 + 5 ÷ 1 = 11	5 − 4 − 1 * 3 * 2 = 0
2 * 3 * 1 ÷ 5 − 4 = -2.8	3 * 2 ÷ 4 − 5 ÷ 1 = -3.5	4 ÷ 2 + 1 * 3 + 5 = 14	5 ÷ 1 * 3 * 2 ÷ 4 = 7.5
2 ÷ 4 − 1 ÷ 5 + 3 = 2.9	3 * 2 + 1 − 4 − 5 = -2	4 ÷ 2 + 1 ÷ 5 + 3 = 3.6	5 ÷ 1 − 4 ÷ 2 * 3 = 1.5
2 ÷ 4 − 1 * 3 + 5 = 3.5	3 * 2 + 1 ÷ 5 − 4 = -2.6	4 − 1 ÷ 5 + 3 * 2 = 7.2	5 + 3 * 2 ÷ 4 − 1 = 3
2 + 1 * 3 + 5 − 4 = 10	3 * 1 ÷ 5 − 4 ÷ 2 = -1.7	4 − 1 + 2 * 3 + 5 = 20	5 + 3 * 1 + 2 ÷ 4 = 2.5
2 + 1 − 4 − 5 + 3 = -3			5 + 3 * 1 − 4 ÷ 2 = 2

The greatest path is 4 − 1 + 2 * 3 + 5 = 20

119

Katherine Johnson Riddle – Key

Why wasn't Katherine Johnson upset she didn't get to go to the moon?

Solve the following problems to find the answer to the riddle. Circle the correct answers in the chart, then solve the riddle.

1. $R + 10 = 4$
2. $M - 5 = -2$
3. $9 \times 0 = -36$
4. $\frac{T}{5} = 14$
5. $-4 + E = -16$
6. $-88 = -8D$
7. $I - (-3) = 19$
8. $C + 11 = 80$
9. $-24 + P = -3$
10. $70 = 2A$
11. $25U = -75$
12. $H + 7 = 15$
13. $\frac{G}{16} = -1$

R	6	-6	14	-14
M	-3	7	3	-7
O	4	3	-5	-4
T	2.5	70	12	19
E	-20	-12	20	12
D	-11	-80	11	80
I	16	22	-22	-16
C	-69	7.5	59	69
P	-21	21	8	-8
A	-35	35	68	72
U	3	50	-3	100
H	22	-8	-22	8
G	-16	16	1	-1

I		C	O	M	P	U	T	E	D
16		69	-4	3	21	-3	70	-12	11

T	H	E		P	A	T	H		T	O
70	8	-12		21	35	70	8		70	-4

G	E	T		T	H	E	R	E
-16	-12	70		70	8	-12	-6	-12

Katherine Johnson Word Search – Key

Find the words that describe the life of Mrs. Katherine Johnson.

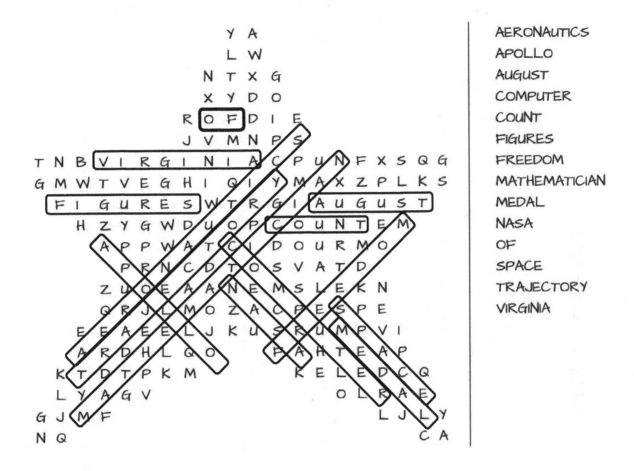

AERONAUTICS
APOLLO
AUGUST
COMPUTER
COUNT
FIGURES
FREEDOM
MATHEMATICIAN
MEDAL
NASA
OF
SPACE
TRAJECTORY
VIRGINIA

Integer Race – Key

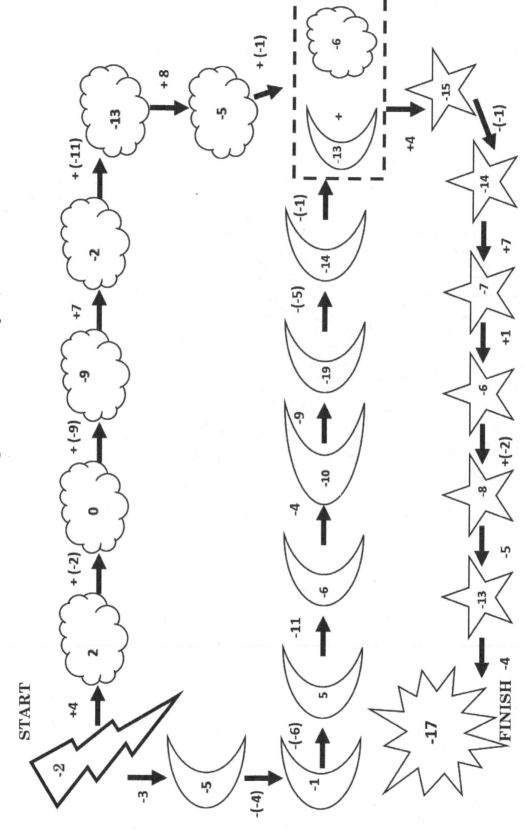

Dr. Tasha Inniss's Message – Key

Do what you love and NEVER GIVE UP when you are following a dream. Perseverance is the key!

Solve the Shapes Puzzle – Key

□ = 4   △ = 2   ○ = 80   ⬡ = 8   ⬠ = 10

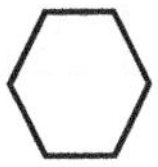

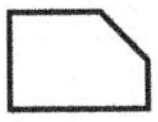

Spatial Statistics Map – Key

1. California

2. Texas

3. Illinois

4. Michigan

5. Ohio

6. Pennsylvania

7. New York

8. Georgia

9. Florida

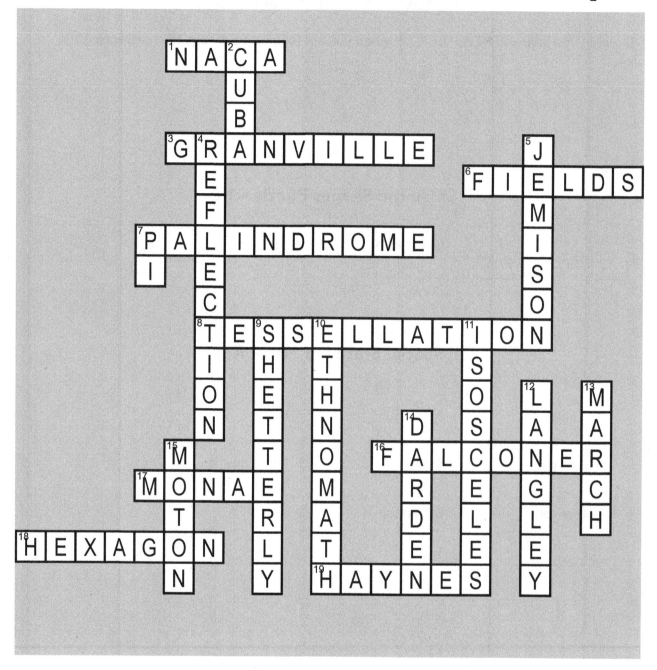

Dr. Taylor Word Search – Key

Directions: The words below are among the many that describe Dr. Shree W. Taylor, as well as some of her interests. Find the words in the word search. Have fun!

research   children   education   environment   health
science   dr taylor   data   solution   help   loyal   spanish   german
mathematics   volunteer   analyst

e	d	u	c	a	t	i	o	n	b	f	j
g	n	a	l	k	w	z	x	p	q	q	m
n	y	v	o	l	u	n	t	e	e	r	a
d	c	h	i	l	d	r	e	n	l	p	t
s	k	u	v	r	e	s	e	a	r	c	h
a	p	t	s	l	o	y	a	l	v	d	e
g	p	a	o	v	x	n	z	g	o	n	m
e	f	b	n	l	c	f	m	a	z	i	a
r	o	c	a	i	k	s	h	e	l	p	t
m	t	t	z	y	s	l	w	q	n	a	i
a	h	t	l	a	e	h	c	a	v	t	c
n	v	o	a	n	o	i	t	u	l	o	s
k	l	t	p	a	n	a	l	y	s	t	d
q	a	m	n	s	c	i	e	n	c	e	c
d	r	t	a	y	l	o	r	u	i	o	v

125

Function Fun Word Search - Key

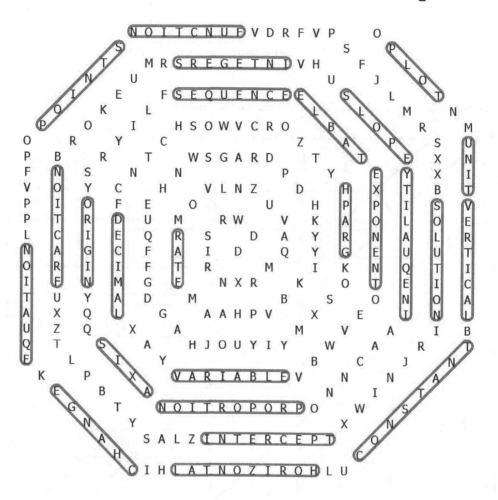

VOCABULARY WORD LIST:

AXIS	FUNCTION	PLOT	TABLE
CHANGE	GRAPH	POINTS	UNIT
CONSTANT	HORIZONTAL	PROPORTION	VARIABLE
DECIMAL	INEQUALITY	RATE	VERTICAL
EQUATION	INTEGERS	SEQUENCE	
EXPONENT	INTERCEPT	SLOPE	
FRACTION	ORIGIN	SOLUTION	

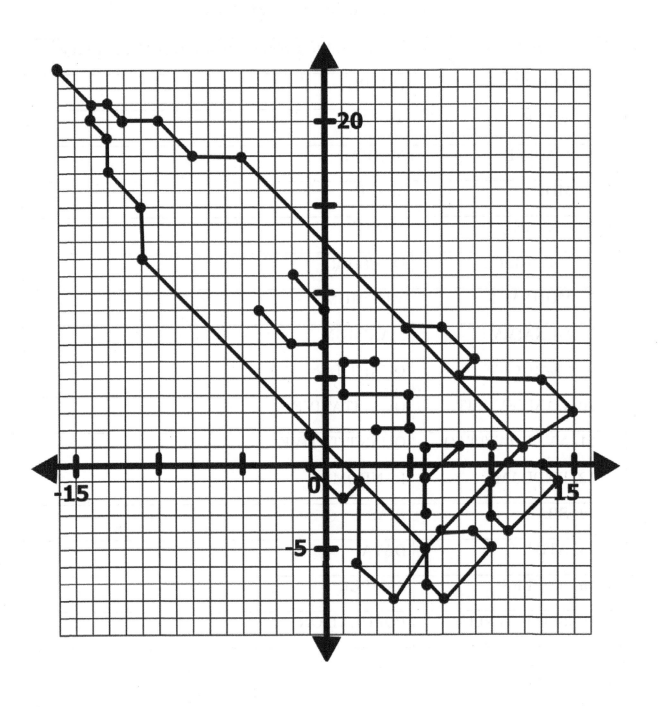

Statistics Words to Know – Key

Please unscramble the words below.

Scrambled Word	Unscrambled Word – Statistics Vocabulary
1. AGHPR	GRAPH
2. MANE	MEAN
3. MADINE	MEDIAN
4. MDEO	MODE
5. GNRAE	RANGE
6. EOTIULR	OUTLIER
7. MUIINMM	MINIMUM
8. MUXAIMM	MAXIMUM
9. LEAIUQRT	QUARTILE
10. QAAITEVULIT	QUALITATIVE
11. NVIEUIATTTAQ	QUANTITATIVE
12. RNDOAM	RANDOM
13. SBAI	BIAS
14. ATDA	DATA
15. AMPLES	SAMPLE
16. PPOAOITNLU	POPULATION

References

[1] American Mathematical Society website. https://www.ams.org/profession/career-info/math-work/math-work, (accessed 10 February 2018).

[2] Eric Addison, Giving Back by the Numbers Gloria Ford Gilmer '49, *Morgan Magazine*, 1 (2011), 16.

[3] Joe Atkinson, *From Computers to Leaders: Women at NASA Langley*, NASA Langley Research Center, Hampton, https://www.nasa.gov/larc/from-computers-to-leaders-women-at-nasa-langley (accessed 11 June 2017).

[4] Robert Q. Berry, III, Mark W. Ellis, Crystal H. Morton, and Jan A. Yow, I Am a Teacher. That's What I've Done Almost All My Life. I Teach. *Journal of Urban Mathematics Education*, 8 (2015), no. 1, 1–9.

[5] Luke Blount, Trailblazer. The story of Baylor's first African-American professor, https://www.bayloralumniassociation.com/baylor_line/past_issues/spr08a_loo.asp, (accessed 23 June 2017).

[6] The Biography.com website, Marjorie Lee Browne, A&E Networks Television, https://www.biography.com/people/marjorie-lee-browne-5602, (accessed 8 June 2017).

[7] The Biography.com website, Euphemia Lofton Haynes Biography, A&E Networks Television, www.biography.com/people/euphemia-lofton-haynes-21465777, (accessed 8 June 2017).

[8] Kristin Block, Gloria Hewitt: Mathematician. *The Mathematics Teacher*, 96 (2003), no. 5, 308.

[9] Viveka Borum and Erica Walker, What Makes the Difference? Black Women's Undergraduate and Graduate Experiences in Mathematics, *The Journal of Negro Education*, Special Focus Topics: Family/Adolescent Studies with Higher Education Studies in Mathematics and Physical Education, 81 (2012), no. 4, 366–378.

[10] CareerCast.com Website, The Best Jobs of 2017, http://www.careercast.com/jobs-rated/best-jobs-2017, (accessed on 10 February 2018).

[11] CollegeBoard.com Website, BigFuture: *Mathematicians*, https://bigfuture.collegeboard.org/careers/computers-math-mathematicians, (accessed 10 February 2018).

[12] Daily Press Obituaries, Dorothy Vaughan http://www.legacy.com/obituaries/dailypress/obituary.aspx?n=dorothy-j-vaughan&pid=120094442, (accessed 7 January 2017).

[13] Daily Press Obituaries, Mary Winston Jackson, http://www.legacy.com/obituaries/dailypress/obituary.aspx?n=mary-winston-jackson&pid=3163015, (accessed 29 December 2016).

[14] Etta Falconer and Lee Lorch, Vivienne Malone-Mayes in Memoriam, *Association for Women in Mathematics (AWM)* Newsletter, 25 (1995), no. 6.

[15] Eric Gillard, *NASA Langley's Hall of Honor Calls 18 Researchers to Join Hallowed Ranks*, NASA Langley Research Center, https://www.nasa.gov/feature/langley/nasa-langley-s-hall-of-honor-calls-18-researchers-to-join-hallowed-ranks, (accessed 11 June 2017).

[16] Jacqueline Giles-Giron, Black pioneers in mathematics: Browne, Granville, Cox, Claytor, and Blackwell, *American Mathematical Society Focus*, 1991, 18.

[17] Nancy A. Gonzales, Merle Mitchell, and Alexander P. Stone, *Mathematical History: Activities, Puzzles, Stories, and Games*, 2nd Edition. National Council of Teachers of Mathematics, Reston, 2001.

[18] Evelyn Boyd Granville, *My Life as a Mathematician*. SAGE: A Scholarly Journal on Black Women, 6 (1989), no. 2, 44–46. Sage Women's Educational Press, Inc.

[19] Derrick Henry, Etta Falconer attracted black women to math. *Atlanta Journal & Constitution Obituaries* in Black Women in Mathematics Website, 2002.

[20] Catherine Hill, Christianne Corbett, and Andresse St. Rose, *Why So Few? Women in Science, Technology, Engineering, and Mathematics*, AAUW: Washington, DC, 2017.

[21] Johnny L. Houston, NAM in *Mathematical Association of America*, www.maa.org/programs/maa-awards/lecture-awards/awm-maa-falconer-lectures/etta-zuber-falconer, (accessed 6 January 2017).

[22] Nicole Hutchison, *Mary Jackson, Introductions Necessary* Website, http://introductionsnecessary.com/2016/04/27/mary-jackson/, (accessed 8 June 2017).

[23] Instructional Fair, Inc., *Crosswords and Wordsearches: Grades 5–8*, Grand Rapids, 1990.

[24] Patricia Clark Kenschaft, Black Men and Women in Mathematical Research. *Journal of Black Studies*, 18 (1987), no. 2, 170–90.

[25] Patricia C. Kenschaft, Black Women in Mathematics in the United States. *American Mathematical Monthly*, 88 (1981), no. 8, 592–604.

[26] Patricia C. Kenschaft, Marjorie Lee Browne: In memoriam, *Association for Women in Mathematics (AWM)* Newsletter, 10 (1980), no. 5, 8–11.

[27] Dr. Knight, Genevieve Madeline Knight. *Mathematical Association of America*, www.maa.org/programs/underrepresented-groups/summa/summa-archival-record/genevieve-madeline-knight, (accessed 17 December 2017).

[28] Genevieve M. Knight, Equity in Mathematics Education: A Set of Conferences. *The Mathematics Teacher*, 77 (1984), no. 3, 235–36.

[29] Evelyn Lamb, Mathematics, Live: A Conversation with Evelyn Boyd Granville. *Scientific American Blog Network*, https://blogs.scientificamerican.com/roots-of-unity/mathematics-live-a-conversation-with-evelyn-boyd-granville/, (accessed 8 June 2017).

[30] Randy Lattimore, Gloria Hewitt: Mathematician, *The Mathematics Teacher*, 94, (2001), no. 1, 9–13, NCTM, Reston.

[31] S.D. Lewis, The Professional Woman: Her Fields have Widened. She Lives with Wind Tunnels. *Ebony*. Johnson Publishing Company. A special issue on the Black woman. XXXII (1977), no. 10. Chicago, https://books.google.com/books?id=08sDAAAAMBAJ&pg=PA116&lpg=PA116&dq=mary+winston+jackson&source=bl&ots=gRjTB-a6bd&sig=wRjwMZGEMb6kHRmYYjCtOONYEbY&hl=en&sa=X&ved=0ahUKEwjSvJqFgcXOAhVJlx4KHR3YA3U4ChDoAQgtMAM#v=onepage&q=mary%20winston%20jackson&f=false, (accessed 8 June 2017).

[32] *Mathematically Gifted and Black website*. http://mathematicallygiftedandblack.com, (accessed 4 September 2017).

[33] Vivienne Mayes, Black and Female, *Association for Women in Mathematics (AWM)* Newsletter, 5 (1975), no. 6, 4–6.

[34] Peggy Mihelich, Women in Mathematics: Professor Sylvia Bozeman. *American Association for the Advancement of Science*, American Association for the Advancement of Science, www.aaas.org/blog/member-spotlight/women-mathematics-professor-sylvia-bozeman, (accessed 7 August 2017).

[35] Vernon R. Morris and Talitha M. Washington, The Role of Professional Societies in STEM Diversity, *Notices of the American Mathematical Society*, 65 (2018), no. 2, 149–155.

[36] Amanda Mylin & Prisca Bird. Vivienne Lucille Malone-Mayes. *Waco History*, Baylor University, www.wacohistory.org/items/show/51, (accessed 31 May 2017).

[37] National Association of Mathematicians (1980). Proceedings of the 11th Annual Meeting, San Antonio, Texas, M. Solveig Espelie, Ed. New York Times 1982.

[38] National Council of Teachers of Mathematics, Genevieve M. Knight: 1999 Lifetime Achievement Award Recipient. http://www.nctm.org/Grants-and-Awards/Lifetime-Achievement-Award/Genevieve-M_-Knight/, (accessed 8 October 2017).

[39] J.J. O'Connor and E.F. Robertson, Evelyn Boyd Granville Biography. MacTutor History of Mathematics Archive, http://www.groups.dcs.stand.ac.uk/~history/Biographies/Granville.html, (accessed 26 December 2016).

[40] Don Robb, *Round Table Geometry: Sir Cumference Classroom Activities*. Charlesbridge Publishing. Watertown, 2010.

[41] Kenneth A. Ross, *Mathematical Association of America Focus*. Interview with Genevieve M. Knight, 18 (2012).

[42] Terri Jo Ryan, (2007/2008). Baylor's First Black Faculty Member, *Waco History Project*, www.wacohistoryproject.org/Moments/vivienne.html.

[43] Margaret R. Sáraco, Historical Research: How to Fit Minority and Women's Studies into Mathematics Class. *Mathematics Teaching in the Middle School*, 14 (2008), no. 2, 70–76. National Council of Teachers of Mathematics, Reston.

[44] M. Shakil, African-Americans in Mathematical Sciences – A Chronological Introduction, *Polygon*, 4 (2010), 27–42.

[45] Rebecca Sharpless, *Oral Memoirs of Vivienne Lucille Malone-Mayes A Series of Interviews*, Baylor University, Institute for Oral History, July/August 1987.

[46] Margot Lee Shetterly, *Dorothy Vaughan Biography*. NASA Page Editor Sarah Loff, https://www.nasa.gov/content/dorothy-vaughan-biography, (accessed 11 June 2017).

[47] Margot Lee Shetterly, *Hidden Figures: The American Dream and the Untold Story of the Black Women Mathematicians Who Helped Win the Space Race*. New York, William Morrow, an Imprint of HarperCollins, 2016.

[48] Tennessee Agricultural and Industrial State University, Faculty Sadie C. Gasaway, *Tennessean 65*, Nashville, 1965.

[49] *The History Makers*. http://www.thehistorymakers.org, (accessed 7 January 2017).

[50] The Journal of Blacks in Higher Education, In Memoriam: Vivienne Malone-Mayes (1932–1995), (1995), no. 9, 104, The JBHE Foundation, Inc.

[51] Lawrence Toppman, The 'Hidden Figure' you still don't know – and she's from Monroe. http://www.charlotteobserver.com/entertainment/ent-columns-blogs/lawrence-toppman/article130289044.html#storylink=cpy, (accessed 12 August 2017).

[52] Eric Vitug, *NACA & NASA Langley Hall of Honor Class of 2017*, Dorothy J. Vaughan, https://www.nasa.gov/langley/hall-of-honor/dorothy-j-vaughan, (accessed 11 June 2017).

[53] Erica N. Walker, *Beyond Banneker: Black Mathematicians and the Paths to Excellence*, State University of New York Press, Albany, 2014.

[54] Wini Warren, *Black Women Scientist in the United States*, Indiana University Press, Bloomington, 1999.

[55]   Scott W. Williams, *Black Women in Mathematics*, The State University of New York at Buffalo, http://www.math.buffalo.edu/mad/PEEPS/womenpeeps.html, (accessed 27 December 2016).

[56]   Website http://www.mazegenerator.net/, (accessed 9 March 2018).

[57]   Website www.mywordsearch.com, (accessed 6 August 2017).

[58]   Website www.crosswordhobbyist.com, (accessed 6 August 2017).

DR. SHELLY M. JONES is an associate professor of mathematics education at Central Connecticut State University in New Britain, Connecticut. She received a B.S. in computer science from Spelman College, an M.S. in mathematics education from the University of Bridgeport, and a Ph.D. in mathematics education from Illinois State University.

Dr. Jones teaches undergraduate mathematics content and methods courses for pre-service teachers as well as graduate-level mathematics content, curriculum, and STEM courses for in-service teachers. Her research interests include culturally relevant mathematics, making connections between mathematics and music, and the effects of college students' attitudes and beliefs about mathematics on their success in college.

Before joining the CCSU faculty, Dr. Jones was a middle school mathematics teacher and a mathematics supervisor in various Connecticut school districts. She was also the assistant director for mathematics at The Project to Increase Mastery of Mathematics and Science (PIMMS) at Wesleyan University in Middletown, Connecticut. Dr. Jones has held talks in Brazil, Ecuador, Bermuda, and the United States. She is a member of various professional organizations including The Benjamin Banneker Association, Inc., The Associated Teachers of Mathematics in Connecticut (ATOMIC), The National Council of Teachers of Mathematics (NCTM), and The National Council of Supervisors of Mathematics (NCSM).

Dr. Jones is a contributing author in the book entitled *The Brilliance of Black Children in Mathematics: Beyond the Numbers and Toward a New Discourse.*

She is the proud parent of two daughters, Brelynn and Brooklynn. She is also a proud member of the Alpha Kappa Alpha Sorority, Incorporated.

VERÔNICA MARTINS is a plastic artist, portraitist, desiġner, painter, teacher, mother, and grandmother. Born in Brazil on September 8, 1957, Verônica Martins received her early foundation in art from her father, and she dedicated many years of her life closely observing how he manipulated pencil on paper and illustrated a world out of which she would eventually emerge.

In December of 2013, the town of Bridgeport, Connecticut, granted Verônica the Artist of the Month Award, due to the proven success and positive influence her art classes provoked in the community. In 2015 and in the consecutive year, she received a trophy for servicing the communities of Connecticut with her art projects dedicated to low-income families.

Today, although Verônica still cannot fully make a living through her art works, when promoting art classes for the communities she can count on the support of some local merchants, as well as the ongoing and unconditional support of the Emanuel-Bridgeport Church, which provides her with a space free of charge for her art classes.

It was a great honor and pleasure to illustrate this book of intelligent women.

Photo Credits

Dr. Christina Eubanks-Turner: Courtesy, Loyola Marymount University

Dr. Raegan Higgins: Texas Tech University

Dr. Tasha R. Inniss: own photo

Dr. Monica Jackson: © Flex in Focus Photography

Dr. Talea Mayo: own photo

Dr. Yolanda Parker: Photograph by Glen E. Ellman

Dr. Candice Price: own photo

Dr. Shree W. Taylor: © Flex in Focus Photography

Dr. Erica N. Walker: Courtesy of Teachers College, Columbia University

Dr. Chelsea Walton: Temple University

Dr. Talitha M. Washington: own photo

Dr. Kimberly S. Weems: own photo

Dr. Shelby Wilson: University of Wisconsin-Eau Claire

Dr. Shelly M. Jones: Photo by Sandy Harden

Veronica Martins: https://www.veronicaartscenter.com/

Tessellations, palindromes, tangrams, oh my! *Women Who Count: Honoring African American Women Mathematicians* is a children's activity book highlighting the lives and work of 29 African American women mathematicians, including Dr. Christine Darden, Mary Jackson, Katherine Johnson, and Dorothy Vaughan from the award-winning book and movie *Hidden Figures*. Although the book is geared toward children in grades 3–8, it is appropriate for all ages.

The book includes portrait sketches and biographies for the featured mathematicians, each followed by elementary-school and middle-school activity pages. Children will enjoy uncovering mathematicians' names in word searches, unscrambling math vocabulary words, solving equations to decode interesting facts, using logical thinking to uncover magic squares, locating hidden objects on an "I Spy" page, and more! They will also read about the important contributions of Drs. Martha Euphemia Lofton Haynes, Evelyn Boyd Granville, and Marjorie Lee Browne, the first three African American women to receive doctoral degrees in mathematics. Other women profiled include contemporary mathematicians who will inspire today's children to become tomorrow's leaders. *Women Who Count* is a must-read for parents and children alike!

I applaud the author's creativity! This activity book is a unique way to expose children early to mathematical ideas and to a part of American history that is not readily accessible at a young age.
Dr. Sylvia T. Bozeman

Realize your "Dream Job". Then work to make that your reality!
Dr. Christine Darden

Diversity of representative images of Black women in all facets of life is so important for all. Thank you to Shelly Jones for providing a platform to celebrate the contributions of Black women to mathematics.
Dr. Candice Price

Once you have learned to think as a mathematician, in a structured and strategic manner, you can solve all kinds of problems. This activity book is the beginning toolbox for aspiring problem solvers!
Dr. Shree Whitaker Taylor

The work Dr. Jones is doing is essential to promoting awareness and inclusion in the mathematical sciences.
Dr. Christina Eubanks-Turner

This is a great endeavor! I'm looking forward to meeting the kids inspired by the book!
Dr. Chelsea Walton

The Euler Paths activity. Love it; a fun challenge.
Teacher

The Quadrilateral Transformations activity has students making predictions and checking their own work. Love this activity!
Teacher